W9-DFT-206

To

From

ADVENTURES IN FATHERHOOD

CARLTON HUGHES and HOLLAND WEBB

Contents

As Different as Night and Day

I will praise You, for I am fearfully and wonderfully made.

PSALM 139:14 NKJV

A well-meaning relative asked my two-year-old son, Noah, "How is your baby brother?" His reply was short and to the point.

"He cries and cries and cries."

My wife and I thought we had the parenting thing down—the first child was so easy. Noah rarely cried and was content to sit on the floor with a pile of books and simple toys, entertaining himself for hours.

Friends tried to warn us: "Wait until you get a second one, it will be so much different than the first!" We dismissed them. How different could another kid be? The joke was clearly on us.

Our second child entered the world three weeks early through a storm of complications and did not breathe on his own at first. The doctor told me Ethan would remain on oxygen for a few hours, but he did not know my little fighter.

My baby boy stayed on the oxygen for half an hour, at which time the nurse said, "Come and get him!" Once he started crying, he hardly stopped for a couple years. Emerging from the long colicky stage, Ethan proved to be our strong-willed child. Stubborn as could be, he was the aggressor in any type of play, and it was not a wise idea to try to take a toy away from him. Noah continued to love books and reading, while Ethan could not sit still long enough to fool with a book.

Through the years, I have learned to appreciate the differences in my boys, who share the same looks but not much else. I am an only child, so my children are my frame of reference for the uniqueness of siblings within the same family.

Like the snowflakes and autumn leaves fashioned by the Creator's hands to be special, each person is unique by design, and I can appreciate the contrasting traits in my sons, knowing they are fearfully and wonderfully made. Noah is crafted in the image of God to carry out an ordained purpose only he can fulfill, and it is the same with Ethan. If we were all the same, life would be boring, so God spiced things up.

—CARLTON

Father, remind me everyone is carefully made in Your image and help me appreciate the differences.

The Botched Execution of the Treasonous Boy

*If any of you lacks wisdom, let him ask of God,
who gives to all liberally and without reproach,
and it will be given to him.*

JAMES 1:5 NKJV

Grandmother!" John-Paul's eyes were wide. "It's Geoffrey! Get the scissors! Hurry!"

My mother rushed to the backyard. My eldest son, Geoffrey, hung from the top of the swing set with a rope around his neck. He grasped his Davy Crockett musket in one hand and clawed at the strand around his neck with the other. The swing bent under his weight as he danced on tiptoe, trying to get free.

I wasn't home, but you can imagine the fear that twisted my gut when I heard about the close call. I had almost lost my son.

"Why," I asked Geoffrey, "did you hang yourself?"

"I was pretending I was British."

"What?!"

"I was being hung for high treason against the Crown. Only I couldn't get the rope off, and I almost got hanged for real."

I wondered again how any of us with a Y chromosome lives to grow up.

I think Geoffrey's role-play incident shaved five years off my life. Being a dad is hard, even harder when you never had anyone to show you how. What do you do when you are faced with the unexpected, dangerous, or downright weird? I couldn't call my dad for advice. Maybe you can't either.

But we can call on God.

This is not God's first parenting rodeo. He is full of wisdom and delights in sharing it with His sons who are trying to be dads. Whether your child is in danger by doing something as nutty as playing make-believe with a real noose or as risky as drugs or crime, God knows how to respond.

Need wisdom for being a father today? Ask God for it. And keep a sharp pair of scissors handy to cut down any treasonous children from their homemade gallows.

—HOLLAND

Father, remind me that Your wisdom is infinitely greater than mine as I seek to be a good father today.

Sorry, Sorry, Sorry

Be kind to one another, tenderhearted, forgiving one another, even as God in Christ forgave you.

EPHESIANS 4:32 NKJV

Noah was two and a half when Ethan was born. He had been the "king"—not only our first child but the first grandchild on both sides of the family. Suddenly he had to share the spotlight with this new addition, and that was not always easy.

When Ethan was a few months old, he and Noah were playing on the floor. Noah took a toy away from baby brother, and predictably, Ethan pitched a big fit. It was a milestone—their first sibling fight. It was before the days of social media, so I apologize for not having a meme or photo to commemorate the event.

"Give the toy back to Ethan and say you're sorry," my wife Kathy instructed Noah.

With shades of things to come, Noah threw the toy at Ethan's feet and, in the most sarcastic voice possible, said "Sorry, sorry, sorry!"

Not exactly what Kathy had in mind. I fought back laughter as she chastised Noah, who was not used to sharing his toys.

We used the situation to talk about asking for forgiveness. God's Word tells us our repentance must be *true* repentance, not just lip service or an act. If we come to the Lord with a repentant, sincere heart, He is faithful and just to forgive us. When we apologize to someone, we must be genuine about it.

Forgiveness seems like a simple thing, but many people cannot understand it. Instead, we hold grudges for years or believe the lie that we cannot be forgiven. In God's economy, however, a sincere "I'm sorry" works, even for brothers.

I would love to say the toy escapade was the last incident of fighting, sarcasm, and subsequent forgiveness between my sons, but I would not want to lie in an inspirational book.

—CARLTON

Father, help me to be quick to forgive others and to be sincere when I need to apologize.

The Copperhead and the King

The king covered his face with his hands and kept on crying, "O my son Absalom! O Absalom, my son, my son!"

2 SAMUEL 19:4 NLT

Someone killed our neighborhood black snake, which was a shame. Black snakes aren't my best friends, but they do keep other vermin in check. Our black snake's death left the local copperhead population unpatrolled.

Now, in case you aren't from the South, let me explain that, while a copperhead's venomous bite isn't likely to leave an adult with a toe tag, it could kill a child. Copperheads are pretty aggressive, too, as snakes go.

One afternoon, my mother went outside to check on my seven- and eight-year-old boys. Seeing the youngest reach for something on the ground, she yelled, "Don't touch that snake!"

He straightened up. "I was just gonna brush the leaves off its back."

The rest of us looked at those copperheads as enemies to be driven away. John-Paul saw only a creature in need of comfort.

What do you see when you look in the face of your angry, defiant, or rebellious child? A child's rebellion can cross a threshold you hadn't dreamed existed. That tiny, wide-eyed darling you'd die for can change in an instant into a sullen, angry, or even violent person who insists on being your enemy. Suddenly, you're sharing a house with someone whose tongue is bitter, whose venom is deadly, and who strikes without warning.

King David's son Absalom had laid plans to wrest the kingdom away from his father through violence. Yet when David heard of his son's death, he mourned for his boy. What does God see when He looks at you and me? A son who laid plans against him? A boy who went his own way? Romans 5:8 NKJV says, "While we were still sinners, Christ died for us."

Look at your rebellious son or daughter with the eyes of your heavenly Father. Can you see a creature in need of comfort? Will you reach out to brush the leaves off your rebellious child's back, even if you know they'll strike you for it?

—HOLLAND

Father, give me Your eyes to see my rebellious child as You see him/her, as a creature in need of Your comfort.

Let Me Tell You Something

Keep on asking, and you will receive what you ask for. Keep on seeking, and you will find. Keep on knocking, and the door will be opened to you.

MATTHEW 7:7 NLT

One Christmas, years ago, when my sons were very young, all Ethan wanted was a football. He was barely old enough to talk, but, for several months, each night after I had tucked the boys into bed and said prayers with them Ethan would motion to me. I would lean down next to him and he would say, "Let me tell you something—I want a football!" His big brother Noah rested in the bed next to Ethan's, seemingly unaffected by little brother's request.

One weekend a few weeks before Christmas, we were enjoying an overnight visit with my parents, and my father joined me for the boys' bedtime ritual. It was the usual pattern—we tucked them in and said their prayers. As I reached to turn off the light, Ethan motioned for my dad to come close.

"Pop, let me tell you something—"

Four-year-old Noah had evidently had all he could take, so he interrupted. "We know! We know! *You want a football!* You've told us a thousand times!"

Night after night, Ethan had made his request, determined to get a football no matter how many times he had to ask, but Noah, frustrated with the whole routine, had heard enough.

I am glad God doesn't get tired of my requests. He doesn't get frustrated and tell me to shut up. Instead, He encourages me to keep asking, to keep seeking, and to keep knocking until He answers. When I tell Him my wants and needs, I'm keeping open the line of communication between the two of us, and that is vital to my growth as a Christian.

For the record, Ethan received three footballs that Christmas, more proof that it pays to ask.

—CARLTON

Father, since You never tire of me asking,
let me tell You something today…

Adventures in Linguistics

A word fitly spoken is like apples of gold in settings of silver.

PROVERBS 25:11 NKJV

We moved to Guatemala when the boys were eight and nine years old. "The people in Guatemala don't speak the same language we do," I repeated 10,372 times before we left. "They speak Spanish."

I didn't realize it, but both boys thought I meant everyone in Guatemala spoke Spanish along with English. They were about to find out differently. On our first full day in Guatemala, I took the boys on a tour of our new town. We stopped for lunch at Pollo Campero, a Guatemalan fried-chicken chain that is to die for.

"Do they have chicken nuggets?" my oldest son asked.

"I can't tell." My Spanish didn't extend that far.

"Ask the waitress," he said.

"You ask."

My son looked our Guatemalan server straight in the eye and in his broad Southern accent said, "Do y'all have chicken nuggets or just chicken strips?"

When the waitress stared at him, my son looked at me quizzically.

"She didn't understand you," I said. "She speaks only Spanish."

The look on his face said he'd finally realized what it meant to live in a country where you can't communicate in English.

Personally, I'm fluent in sarcasm. My kids don't understand that any better than our Guatemalan waitress understood Southern American English. But it doesn't stop me from believing that somehow a bitter tongue will produce a sweet fruit.

It won't.

The Bible has a lot to say about our language, much more than "don't cuss" and "don't lie." Scripture encourages us to build each other up, to speak life-giving words that bring healing to the weak and turn away the wrath of the strong. Are you up for learning a new language?

—HOLLAND

Father, help me speak with grace and wisdom.

America the Beaut

Your word I have hidden in my heart,
that I might not sin against You.

PSALM 119:11 NKJV

As a toddler, Ethan had a special talking/singing book that he listened to all the time. One of the book's options dealt with Americana music—an odd choice for a two-year-old's entertainment, but, for whatever reason, it worked.

Ethan's favorite song in the book was "America the Beautiful," only he sang it like this: "America! America! America the Beaut!"

No matter what verse or refrain, he lifted up his voice with those words. No amber waves, no purple mountain majesties, just "America the Beaut." All day, every day.

One day I was playing around with the family video camera—a big, clunky number that recorded on VHS tape—and I asked Ethan to sing his "America the Beaut" number so I could record it for posterity.

"No, I want to sing the *Clifford* song!"

His favorite television show at the time was *Clifford the Big Red Dog*, and he would hum the theme song with each viewing. Even though I had never heard him sing the lyrics, I agreed and pressed record.

"Okay, sing the *Clifford* song," I said.

Panic came over his face. "Wait, I don't know it!"

I suppressed my laughter as he broke into "America the Beaut," belting it out with great abandon. That encounter became a favorite scene from his childhood.

Just as Ethan could not sing something he had not memorized, I have trouble dealing with life when I have not hidden God's Word in my heart. Studying the Bible and remembering its verses gives me protection and refuge when I need them. In times of spiritual warfare, God's Word is my weapon. Am I afraid? I think of verses featuring "Fear not." Down in my spirit? I remember the promises in Psalms. Facing a trial? I recite verses about God's victory in our battles.

However, if I'm feeling patriotic, I don't say a verse. I sing "America the Beaut," of course.

—CARLTON

Father, show me the verses You want me to hide in my heart, so I will be ready for what life throws at me.

There will always be
the unknown.
There will always be
the unprovable.
But faith confronts those
frontiers with a thrilling leap.
Then life becomes vibrant
with adventure!

ROBERT SCHULLER

Loving the Mismatched

God sets the lonely in families.

PSALM 68:6 NIV

How do I explain that I have two sons, one nephew, and two nieces, but I have no wife and no siblings?

It works like this. My parents had one child, and since they achieved perfection with that one (me), they didn't need any more. Or at least, that's the story I tell myself. Anyway I'm an only child. When I was a kid, my mother's best friend also had an only child, a girl named Amanda. The first time I met Amanda, I begged my mother not to make me visit "that awful little girl" again. Now, thirty-five years later, we consider one another family. God does tricky things sometimes.

Amanda grew up, married, adopted two children, birthed one, and has generally succeeded beyond anyone's wildest expectations. Her children are how I came to have two nieces and a nephew. Like Amanda, I also grew up (sort of), but I didn't marry. I did, however, adopt two boys while I was in my twenties. That's how I came to have two sons.

So I have no wife and no siblings but two sons, one nephew, and two nieces. The five of them represent four races, three countries, and three languages. All of us out to dinner together would probably look like a working group from the United Nations. We're a bit mismatched, not related by blood but made into family by choice and by grace.

Many of us these days are missing parts of our families. We're like a puzzle with pieces missing here and there and others from different boxes tossed in as replacements.

God can put the puzzle of a family together in ways that don't make sense to us but that look right and good when He's done. No matter how mismatched your relatives seem to be, God can set a strong and loving family around you. That's what it means to be one of His people—loved not just by God but by the family of God as well.

—HOLLAND

Father, thank You that You have set me in a family—not only the family related to me, but Your family as well.

Make and Model

My sheep hear My voice, and I know them,
and they follow Me.

JOHN 10:27 NKJV

One day when Noah was barely old enough to talk, my father walked him to the car and showed him the symbol on the back.

"It's a Chevrolet," my dad explained.

It became a ritual for them to examine cars and their symbols. If we went out to eat or to shop with my parents, Dad and my son would walk around outside the place, looking at different types of cars. By the time Noah was three, he could tell you the make and model of most any vehicle.

Road trips were interesting, as Noah would peer out the window the whole time. "I see a Ford Windstar! There's a Chevy Cavalier like Mamaw Sue and Pop's! Nanna and Poppy drive a Buick like that one!" His imaginary friend Kelsey even drove a Mustang.

A man at church was skeptical of my son's knowledge, so one Sunday, he insisted on quizzing Noah as they walked around the parking lot. Noah named not only the make and model of every car but the person who owned each one. The man was dumbfounded and never doubted my boy again.

Noah had been taught to recognize cars by their symbols. How do we recognize God's voice?

Jesus is my Shepherd; He guides me, a lost sheep, through this crazy life. There are times I do not know which way to turn, but if I listen closely, I will hear my Shepherd leading me in the right direction.

Noah learned the types of cars after much examination; similarly, it takes a while to discern the Lord's voice. Sometimes I feel a nudge as I read His Word. Other times I hear a quiet voice beckoning me to do (or not do) something. I even sense Him in the sounds of nature—in the wind or in the rolling creek near my church.

I cannot say I have heard Him through a car symbol, but I am open to the possibility.

—CARLTON

Lord, teach me to hear Your voice in different ways and to know it is You.

Are We Christians?

Agrippa interrupted him. "Do you think you can persuade me to become a Christian so quickly?"

ACTS 26:28 NLT

From the start, I schlepped the boys to everything we could get into at church. They attended Sunday school morning services, parties, and musicals. In the summer, they showed up at every Vacation Bible School from the charismatics to the Lutherans. Summertime meant a theological smorgasbord for the boys and peaceful nights at home for me.

We also read Christian books, memorized Bible verses learned the creeds, attended Christian schools, and consumed faith-based media. Imagine my surprise when one day my oldest son, about ten years old at the time, piped up. "We go to the Nazarene church. Does that mean we're Christians, or are we something else?"

To my credit, I swallowed back my first response, which was, "No, dude, we're Hindus." Instead, I emailed the children's minister and asked for a refund.

Seriously? How could he miss this?

Guys, here's the hardest thing I've learned so far in life nobody was ever parented into the kingdom of God. Nobody gets a special dispensation to enter heaven based on how many Bible verses they've memorized. On the road of faith nobody gets to bypass a transforming encounter with grace.

The grace of God reaches down to us. We must realize we are sinners, utterly devoid of hope, and we must reach back in faith. That's how God draws us into His family.

Dad, if your plan is to growth-hack your child's salvation through church attendance and a Christian upbringing, then your plan will fail. The kingdom of God does not offer a separate entrance for boys and girls who've recited their memory verses without error. It offers only one way home. No other path, not even one marked "Christian," will get you there.

Salvation comes by grace alone through faith alone in Christ alone. Anything less is a religious delusion.

—HOLLAND

Father, in my desire to nurture my children in faith, help me not to stand in the way of Your grace.

Will This Be on the Test?

Do not forget to entertain strangers, for by so doing some have unwittingly entertained angels.

HEBREWS 13:2 NKJV

Growing up, my sons had the pleasure of their dad being their children's pastor. I'm sure they were thrilled. One Sunday, my children's sermon concerned entertaining angels unaware—how God will occasionally place someone who needs help in your path to see if you will answer the call. It was a riveting message.

Well, it was riveting to me. The kids, on the other hand, were their usual selves, squirming in their seats, requesting snacks, and asking when all the talking would be over so they could play with toys. It was a typical day in the life of a children's pastor. When church ended, I was ready to head home for my Sunday afternoon nap, but, first, I had to stop at the grocery store.

Kathy was at home, sick, but had given me a list of things we needed. We arrived at the store and, as I was helping Noah and Ethan out of the car, a young woman approached us.

"Please, sir, I don't have any money, and I need food for my children. Will you help?"

The boys' eyes grew as big as saucers as they looked to see how their dad/children's pastor would respond. As a general ule, I don't just hand people money in situations like this one, ut I do try to help in some way.

I thought fast and told the lady I would give money to ne of the cashiers so she could get what she needed. Not o coincidentally, a girl whose family attended our church vas working one of the lines. I gave her the money, and the oung woman was satisfied and went off to get her groceries. Ve purchased our items and back in the car, the boys were stounded.

"Dad, we *just* learned about helping others, and *this lady hows up*!"

Not only did the experience reinforce the children's ser-non, it was also a prime opportunity for me to talk about esting. I explained that when we study God's Word, He wants o know we are taking the lessons to heart, to see if we will live ut what we have read.

We never know when we will entertain angels, and we lso don't know ahead of time when we will be tested. It pays o be ready for a pop quiz.

—CARLTON

Father, may I be ready when Your Word tests me.

This Little Light of Mine

Your word is a lamp to my feet and a light to my path.

PSALM 119:105 NKJV

When I was in my late twenties, my mother worried that I would never marry. Once she cheered herself up by saying, "Well, your dad was sixty-five when you were born, so I guess genetics means you'll still be able to get married for a long time to come." I died. Deep down, I feared I wouldn't find the right girl. And now even my mom had doubts?

Even weirder than becoming a dad at sixty-five was the assortment of things my dad had collected throughout his life. Normal stuff for his generation, I guess, but weird when compared to other people's dads' stuff. Like the tiny oil lamp with a hook for a fingerhold. When my dad was a little boy, more than a hundred years ago now, his family lived out in the country in southern Kentucky. No one had electricity, indoor bathrooms, or outside lights then. At night, the path to the outhouse door could feel terrifying, especially to a child. My dad would light that tiny oil lamp, turn up the wick, and head for the outhouse—in the pitch dark. The lamp had no glass hurricane to shield the flame, so Dad had to use his hand. That blocked the light from the path, of course. But

he would fix his eyes on that tiny light the whole trip to the outhouse and back, too terrified to look away from the light at the darkness all around. No wonder Dad kept that lamp as a reminder of how important a light can be in the dark.

How dark is your world? Is your path obscured? Is the darkness terrifying? Focus on the flame in front of you. The light of God, which the Bible says came into the world through Jesus, might feel frail and look small, but that's only your imagination. In fact, God's light shines brightly, invading the darkest places of life with the glow of His grace.

—HOLLAND

Father, when life grows pitch dark,
fix my eyes on Your light.

Of Bikes and Boys and Direction

I have stayed on God's paths; I have followed his ways and not turned aside.

JOB 23:11 NLT

Growing up, I was a clumsy kid. Coordination was simply not my thing, and I was always tripping over my own huge feet. Even something like tying my shoes was a struggle to learn. Noah was a lot like me—not the most graceful child, to put it nicely. Teaching him to ride a bicycle was a bit of a challenge.

We lived in a crowded neighborhood with narrow sidewalks. It was not the best place for bicycles. The large, open parking lot at the community college where I worked, however, was a perfect place to ride in the off-hours, so one evening, Kathy and I loaded up the bikes and our boys and drove them to the college for a lesson.

We unloaded, and I spent some time coaching each boy and walking them through a ride. Ethan quickly picked up the skill of riding without training wheels and sped off making several laps on his own, but Noah required more effort and practice. After many starts and stops, he finally got the hang of it. He pedaled up to speed and cruised through the lot with ease as Kathy and I cheered him on. Then it happened.

In that expansive space with plenty of room to ride, Noah ooled toward one of the few light poles there and rammed into it. Thankfully, he was okay—he picked himself up and raced off again, but ever since, we have teased him about his ability to find the one obstacle in an otherwise clear area.

How many times have I been on the right path with God only to hit a "light pole" and slow my progress? At times, I've gotten ahead of Him on the path, jumping into things I was not yet ready for. Other times, I've hesitated to follow God's leading and missed a blessing.

While parenting is hard, slowly but surely, I have learned to take God's direction. He is my guide, and I realized, if I sought Him first, He would keep me on the right path and help me dodge those big obstacles.

—CARLTON

Father, You lead, and I will follow today.

There is something ultimate in a father's love, something that cannot fail, something to be believed against the whole world.

FREDERICK W. FABER

Wait

I will wait for the God of my salvation;
my God will hear me.

MICAH 7:7 NKJV

About 9 p.m. one Sunday night when my oldest son wa in fourth grade, he popped into the kitchen with ai announcement. "I forgot to tell you that I said you'd bak cookies for my class's bake sale tomorrow morning at 7:30. I delivered a poorly received speech about timeliness and re sponsibility. It was a good speech, filled with wise sayings anc truisms; in fact, I'd given it so many times, I had it memo rized. So did he, by the way, but it never did any good. Still, gave it again out of habit.

Did I question him to be sure the bake sale was tomor row? Did I pray for direction—whether to let this go o bulldoze ahead? No. All I had to do was push hard, and I'c fix this. I checked the cupboards. No brown sugar or vanill flavoring. Since we lived in Guatemala at the time, it wasn't matter of popping across the street. Grumbling and snarling I bundled my oldest into my truck and drove through a mas sive downpour to a store with imported goods.

Back home, we mixed the cookies, only to discover w had also run out of gas to power the oven. The gas compan didn't open until 9:00 the next morning.

I shoved the cookie batter into the fridge, made anothe speech, and set my alarm to get up an hour early. That way we could get to the kitchen in the building where I worked at the school and bake the cookies before 7:30. All went as planned. I was making this happen. Minutes before that early morning deadline, I was drawing warm, chocolatey cookies from the oven.

I shoveled them into containers and thrust them into my son's hands. "Go."

A few minutes later, he came slinking back. "The bake sale's next week."

Ever gotten your timing off? Done something too early? The Bible uses the word "wait" something like 140 times. But waiting feels so counterintuitive. So I move heaven and earth, only to discover my efforts were pointless. I should've waited on God first. Are there any areas in your parenting where you could do the same?

—HOLLAND

*Father, give me the grace to wait on
Your timing before I act.*

Rodent Lunch of Terror

There is no fear in love; but perfect love casts out fear.

1 JOHN 4:18 NKJV

When my boys were very young, they saw commercials about a certain kid-friendly restaurant named after a giant rodent. As we planned a trip to the big city to visit their uncles, my sons had one request.

"We want to eat lunch with that mouse!"

It sounded like a good treat for them, so Kathy and I arranged for our relatives to meet us at the restaurant. During the long car ride, the boys repeated the same phrase over and over.

"We're going to eat lunch with that mouse!"

The place was crowded when we arrived, so we searched for a table before we ordered our food. As we were getting seated, the aforementioned rodent—an employee in a big furry suit—appeared out of nowhere to greet the children. Many kids squealed with delight. My boys? They took one look and screamed uncontrollably.

"Ahh! Get it away from me!"

"I don't want that thing around me! Get me out of here!"

The whole restaurant watched as we scooped up the boys and made a beeline to the exit. It was one of those experiences hat was funny and horrific at the same time. We waited a few years before we tried to eat there again and once the fear of "that mouse" had passed, the restaurant became one of their favorite places during the rest of their childhood.

Fear can stop us dead in our tracks and keep us from enjoying the life God has placed before us. I cringe as I look back at the adventures I have missed because I was too afraid to go. I must remind myself that fear is a liar, but the truth of God is the antidote. His perfect love casts fear away and frees me to live an exciting life in Him.

If we believe God when He tells us to "fear not," the adventure, and restaurant possibilities, are endless.

—CARLTON

Father, remind me You are with me on all my adventures, so I don't have to be afraid.

Horses, Westerns, and Bad Decisions

The wise are cautious and avoid danger;
fools plunge ahead with reckless confidence.

PROVERBS 14:16 NLT

We dads weren't always the sage advice givers we are now. Some of us took part in some serious shenanigans of our own.

I'm not gonna tell you any of mine, but Pop, my maternal grandfather who is now deceased, will not mind my sharing his.

Sometime around 1934, a new movie theater came to our small town in southern Kentucky. Townsfolk couldn't wait for Saturday afternoon to watch those cowboys and bandits gallop across the screen in jerky black-and-white motion pictures.

It was on one such day that Pop, who was just a young adult at the time, spied a horse tethered on the town square. (For purposes of this story, let me just say that I don't think Pop was 100 percent sober that day.)

Pop untied the horse, clambered up on its back, and rode it around the square. Then he saw the movie theater. Pop rode that horse into the darkened auditorium and down the center aisle.

Flickering lights and sounds terrified the animal, which promptly went berserk at the front of the theater. After several minutes, Pop and the theater owner—who, in a weird twist of fate, would later be my dad—got the horse outside, where it galloped at full speed all the way to the river. I don't know if Pop faced any consequences for his actions, but he probably didn't. His family was known for doing outlandish things.

Your kids are bound to pull some zany stunts too. They'll probably laugh about them one day when they're entertaining the other residents in the senior-citizen home, just like Pop did. But before you open your mouth to respond to them, pause and think. What did people say and do after some of your shenanigans? How did their words and actions affect you?

You get one chance to teach a powerful lesson in situations like these—and sometimes the one that impacts them most is showing a little mercy.

—HOLLAND

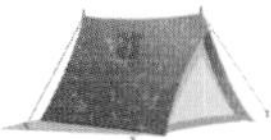

Father, give me Your perspective to deal with my kids' foolishness.

A Close Shave

Jesus Christ is the same yesterday, today, and forever.

HEBREWS 13:8 NKJV

Growing facial hair has been a talent of mine for decades. I had to start shaving when I was in seventh grade, the first boy in the entire class to do so, and I have worn a full-blown beard for most of the last thirty years. I like the convenience of not having to shave every day, as my five-o'clock shadow tends to appear by 9 a.m. My wife also prefers the look, not to mention the double chin it hides, so beard it is.

My sons had never seen me clean-shaven until one day when they were just past the toddler stage. I got a "wild hair," as we say here in Kentucky, and spontaneously decided to get rid of the beard. When I emerged from the bathroom with my naked face, my boys were in shock.

Ethan studied my bare mug with a look of terror. "You're not my dad!"

Noah was blunt with his order, pointing to the bathroom. "Go back in there and put the beard back on!"

Obviously, my hairless look was a failed experiment, so I avoided the razor for the next few days and soon had significant facial hair growth—much grayer this time, I might add. Before long, Noah and Ethan had their fuzzy-faced dad back.

Change is inevitable in life, yet I don't like it. I prefer he status quo, I enjoy things as they are without much variation—but that's not how God envisions my life. He knows hings in this world of chaos are constantly changing, and I am witnessing that fact lately in different areas of life: my day ob, my home life, my church.

I am thankful for the one constant in my life who never changes: Jesus. When life's circumstances turn upside down, I can count on Him to be there, calming me and assuring me through the topsy-turvy situation. Change doesn't have to be a bad thing, all I need to remember is that God is in control.

Who knows? Maybe I'll even try shaving again. Hmm… nah!

—CARLTON

Father, be my constant and calm me when changes come.

Why Can't I Have a Dragon?

I will be a father to him, and he'll be a son to me.
When he does wrong, I'll discipline him in the usual ways,
the pitfalls and obstacles of this mortal life.
But I'll never remove my gracious love from him.

2 SAMUEL 7:14–15 MSG

Birth control is not 100 percent effective. No matter what the experts say, I'm living proof that a pill a day does not always keep a baby away.

My parents planned to live a child-free existence, because my dad was already an old man and my mother didn't much like children. When she told her coworkers that she was pregnant, they took bets on how long I would last in her care, telling her, "there's not a maternal bone in your body."

Somehow, though, I managed to survive to adulthood. I did it without my dad, however, who died when I was a child. It's bizarre to me that I'm writing a book about being a dad. In his book, *To Own a Dragon: Thoughts on Growing Up without a Father*, Donald Miller writes, "I feel as though I'm writing a book about a troll under a bridge or a dragon. For me, a father was nothing more than a character in a fairy tale. As a kid, I wondered why I couldn't have a dragon, but I never wondered why I didn't have a father."

Today, fifteen million American children are growing up n homes without fathers, a statistic I can hardly bear to think bout. Millions more live with fathers like me who, because ve never had anyone to show us, have no idea what we're loing.

How can you be a good dad when you didn't have one any nore than you had a pet dragon?

You can ask God for wisdom. Throughout Scripture, God gave men and women the wisdom they needed to do the vork required of them. Speaking from experience, I can tell ou that God will provide the wisdom you need to be a dad, vhether through the life of your own dad or in some other vay. Just ask.

—HOLLAND

Father, my own dad may not have offered the model of fatherhood I needed, so I ask You for wisdom to parent my children in ways that honor You.

Dad, I Wanna Go!

And the King will answer and say to them, "Assuredly, I say to you, inasmuch as you did it to one of the least of these My brethren, you did it to Me."

MATTHEW 25:40 NKJV

There's something I need to confess about my family—we have an addiction.

We cannot stop packing shoeboxes.

When my boys were toddlers, I felt called to coordinat the Operation Christmas Child shoebox ministry at ou church. We had humble beginnings that first year—we fille thirty-seven boxes with fun and useful items to be sent t needy children around the globe. Now we regularly pack ove five hundred boxes at our small, rural location. Come packin time in November, both our house and church look like dolla stores gone awry, and every member, from two to eighty-tw gets involved.

When Ethan was seven, he and I were running some er rands and stopped at the church to add some items to ou shoebox stockpile. As we were storing stuffed animals an washcloths, Ethan, out of the blue, said "Dad, I wanna go!"

I figured he wanted to get back to his toys and vide games. "Be patient, son, we'll go home in a few minutes."

"No, Dad, I wanna *go*!" There was a different, urgent ton to his voice. "I wanna go to one of these countries and giv out shoeboxes to kids someday."

It was a heavenly *a-ha* moment for me. I realized my son understood what true Christian love looked like; he'd connected with Jesus's admonition that good deeds directed to the "least of these."

Ethan has developed over the years into a caring, compassionate young man. He's the one who takes care of the younger children at family gatherings, the one who reaches out to those who need a friend. It will not surprise me if someday he ends up going to give out shoeboxes in a faraway land or to do other good deeds in the name of Jesus.

Compassion does not automatically appear in children—they learn by example. The years of packing and lugging shoeboxes taught Ethan—and the other kids at our church—about Christian love in action.

Don't you wanna go?

—CARLTON

Father, let Your love and compassion be evident in my children.

I Wish I Had It in Me

Watch, stand fast in the faith, be brave, be strong.
Let all that you do be done with love.

1 CORINTHIANS 16:13–14 NKJV

My oldest son does manly things. He's a beast, a fast-paced, muscle-bound animal who jumps out of airplanes for the US Army for a living. Every new place he goes, the army offers him a leadership role.

My own dad also served in the Army Airborne and fought in a war where his job was to identify corpses after a battle. He later served as a judge and county executive.

My grandfather enlisted in World War I as a medic. Given the brutality of that conflict, I can't even imagine what he had to do.

These three make up my idea of great men. Watchful men. Firm men. Strong men.

Me, on the other hand? Well, I run an online communication business. Getting a testy email from a client is about as dangerous as my job gets. At times, my work doesn't even remotely feel like a manly thing to do. It's certainly not jumping out of planes or identifying corpses on a battlefield.

What does it mean to be a man, anyway? How do I measure up as a Christian man? How do I teach my sons to be men?

Your high school biology teacher probably answered the first question. Paul answered the second and third questions n today's Scripture: Be watchful, stand firm in the faith, act ike men, be strong. Whatever you do, do it in love.

Watchful. Firm. Strong. Love. These characteristics make a godly man.

Are you watchful? Do you keep an eye out for where the enemy could attack your family?

Are you firm? Do your kids know they can depend on you to do what you say you'll do? How about strong? Are you he man who knows how to "bear all things," as 1 Corinthians 13:7 says? Do you act in love?

Regardless of your occupation, these are the key questions of masculine identity. Now, if you'll excuse me, I have some testy clients to handle.

—HOLLAND

Father, give me strength to act like the man You made me to be today.

Much of what is sacred
is hidden in the ordinary,
everyday moments of our lives.
To see something of the sacred
in those moments takes
slowing down so we can live
our lives more reflectively.

KEN GIRE

Not in My House

My eyes have seen Your salvation, which You have prepared before the face of all peoples.

LUKE 2:30–31 NKJV

There's nothing like seeing Christmas through the eyes of a child, and as much as Kathy and I tried to keep Christ at the center of the holiday, there was always much excitement about the presents.

Like many Christian families, we wondered how to handle the issue of Santa Claus. In the end, decided to roll with it. Many gifts came from Mom and Dad, but a few special ones arrived on Christmas morning, courtesy of the jolly old elf.

One Christmas Eve, I tucked the boys into bed and reminded them, "The sooner you go to sleep, the sooner Santa will come with your presents."

Ethan lost it. "I don't want that man in my house! Don't let him come in!" He cried so hard, he could barely talk and breathe.

Older brother Noah tried to console him. "Santa doesn't *really* come into our house!"

Sooner than we expected, Kathy and I gave them "the talk" about who was real and who wasn't, and Ethan calmed down. Both boys were fine once they saw their haul under the tree the next morning.

At an after-Christmas clearance sale, we found a book for children about Saint Nicholas and how he was a real person with a generous spirit. The author encouraged children to think of him when they see someone in a red suit with a white beard. The message resonated with my boys, and we never again had a problem on Christmas.

Mind you, there are families where Santa isn't an issue, and that's fine. But our ordeal taught me the importance of being honest with my children, even at that young age. I realized I did not have to tell my sons everything, but I did need to be truthful in manners affecting them. Jesus said the truth will set you free, and it did with the Santa escapade.

Our lessons about the real meaning of the holiday replaced the fear of a chubby, bearded stranger entering our house with a realization of the love and generosity of God that made Christmas possible.

Plus, it was no longer a secret who ate the cookies under the tree, so I found many of my favorites waiting for me in the years that followed. I call that a win-win for everyone.

—CARLTON

Father, may my children dwell in the truth of Your love.

I Have Other Plans

There are "friends" who destroy each other,
but a real friend sticks closer than a brother.

PROVERBS 18:24 NLT

When the boys were little, our family friend Tonya would visit frequently. She served as a social worker and often volunteered in children's ministry, but she had no children of her own, so I let her borrow mine. Tonya loved to tease the kids, and the boys enjoyed dishing it back out to her. She did a lot for us, and I wanted her to know how much we appreciated her efforts. So one February morning, I said, "Do you know what makes today special?"

Geoffrey, who had just turned nine years old, said, "It's Ms. Tonya's birthday!"

If he does as well with anniversaries, he'll make an awesome husband one day. But I digress.

"Yes, it's her birthday," I said. "We must do something nice for her this weekend."

John-Paul, fresh off his eighth birthday, replied, "I already have other plans."

I laughed, and of course, he couldn't wait for me to tell Ms. Tonya about his "witty" remark. Tonya knew John-Paul's quirky sense of humor, so she laughed too. It reminded me, though, of how easy it is to destroy a friend. A lighting shaft of humor can seem witty in my head but sound mean-spirited when it comes out of my mouth.

The Bible has much to say about how we talk to our friends. The same truths apply to how we speak to our families. Dad, how do you talk to your kids? Do they laugh because you're funny? Or do they laugh to wipe away the hurt from your stinging "wit"? I've learned the hard way that a dad's words, once spoken, can't be retracted. And they can cause major damage. The good news is that words of encouragement, support, and love also have powerful effects. So if your words haven't been what you'd like them to be, you can change. Start today with a word of encouragement at breakfast.

—HOLLAND

Father, help me speak words of encouragement to my family and friends and keep me from using humor as an excuse for being hurtful.

Ethan's Uno Challenge

I press toward the goal for the prize of the upward call of God in Christ Jesus.

PHILIPPIANS 3:14 NKJV

I have never been one to let kids win a game just because they're kids. I want to win! Seriously, how are children going to learn the game and a spirit of healthy competition if we let them win all the time?

My grandmother, whom I called Mamaw, taught me this principle during overnight stays at her house throughout my childhood. Sure, she made me homemade gingerbread and fed me unlimited snacks like any other doting grandparent would do. But don't let that sweet facade fool you—she also beat me unmercifully at 500 Rummy for years. My losing streak ended when, at the ripe old age of thirteen, I finally won a game. Mamaw had a great response.

"Now I know I've taught you the game well," she said.

One winter evening, my son Ethan challenged me to a game of Uno. I agreed and soundly beat him. He is competitive (obviously it runs in our family) and wanted to play again, so we did. I won that game too. And another. And another. I beat him fourteen straight times, but he wouldn't give up. Finally, on the fifteenth try, he beat me.

He was defeated fourteen times, but Ethan didn't give

ıp—he pressed on until he finally tasted victory. I admired ıis tenacity. God wants us to have a "can do, never give up" pirit when we are living and working for Him.

For fourteen years, I tried to get a book published until ı company finally trusted me with the one you are holding n your hands. I cannot count the times I wanted to quit, but 3od would not let me.

In pressing toward the mark, as the Bible calls it, we de- 'elop a spirit of perseverance, a determination that will get us hrough the battles of this life. The call of Jesus is not the easy vay, but it will be worth it in the end.

—CARLTON

Father, give me the strength to persevere and to press on for You.

Addicted to "Gua-del-mo-del"

Do not worry about tomorrow.

MATTHEW 6:34 NKJV

A few years ago, I bought a house. It's the twenty-third home I've lived in since I was born, not counting short-term situations. That's a lot of houses and a lot of moving.

Over the years, I've gotten pretty good at relocating. The secret is to get rid of almost everything you own. It's a lot easier to move with light baggage than it is to haul truckloads of belongings around.

Some of my relocations have sparked more excitement than others. I've lived abroad twice, and those moves were exciting. A few others were sparked out of wrenching changes and I am glad not to relive those.

Over the years, though, I've learned to enjoy moving. It involves some changing, some leaving things behind. But moving also means new friendships, fresh discoveries, and exciting adventures.

We moved to Guatemala in 2009, and I'll admit, I was a little nervous about it. For one thing, neither boy could pronounce "Guatemala" correctly. The word came out something like "Gua-del-mo-del." I have since discovered it is not necessary to know a country's name in order to successfully live there.

But more to the point, I worried how my middle-class American kids would react to the piles of trash, the shoe-shine boys, the street kids, and the general poverty amid the country's warmth and beauty. I wondered what they'd think of the Guatemalan ladies who clucked over them in public. I worried that they'd want to return to the United States and to the life we'd had when they saw the reality in front of them.

I worried in vain. In a promotional video for their school in Guatemala, Geoffrey said, "I love it here. I have loads of friends." He later told me, "After a while, you get addicted to life in Guatemala."

Our three years there turned out to be the best years of our lives together. Ironically, all my worrying was focused on the wrong thing. When we left Guatemala, I was confident the boys would love our next adventure.

As dads, we know a lot, but we don't know the future. I'm thankful for an all-knowing Father into whose hands I can trust the future without worrying about it.

—HOLLAND

Father, help me to trust Your plans and not to worry.

Sample and See

Oh taste and see that the L*ORD* *is good;*
blessed is the man who trusts in Him!

PSALM 34:8 NKJV

Once boys hit the preteen years, their stomachs are bottomless pits. Our grocery bill increased by leaps and bounds when my sons reached that stage. But whenever we visited the "big city," I had a solution for their hunger pangs: samples at the warehouse club store. I would cut them loose in the food department with the instruction to "sample away!"

You name it, and they tried it—granola bars, cheesecake, fresh-squeezed orange juice, pizza, and every type of chicken nugget/strip/patty imaginable. On one visit, we encountered something different: samples of lamb.

I have always been the primary cook at our house, but I have never made lamb. Not only was I a picky eater growing up, but I also loved watching Shari Lewis and her puppet Lamb Chop. You will understand why I could not fathom eating something so cute and cuddly. My boys, however, were eager to try it. As we walked around, they munched and weighed in with their opinions.

"This is great!"

"I love it! Let's buy some lamb and make it at home!"

I was not about to buy a lamb to cook at home, thank you very much, but I was glad my sons were expanding their alates. I'd always told them they would never know if they ked something until they tasted it.

It was the same way with Jesus. How would my sons ever now about the Savior if I did not take them to church to aste and see, as the Bible proclaims in Psalm 34:8, that He good? Noah and Ethan would tell you they had a drug roblem growing up—I drug them to church every time the oors opened.

There's a second part of that verse too, that promises we vill be blessed if we trust in Jesus. I wanted to give my sons very opportunity to do that, and I am pleased that both of hem are Christians, serving in churches where they live. Just s they sampled the food and declared it good, they have asted and seen that the true Lamb is good.

—CARLTON

Father, may my children come to know that You are good, and may they continue to put their trust in You.

Calling Out That Name

The Lord *is close to all who call on him,*
yes, to all who call on him in truth.

PSALM 145:18 NLT

I love getting away from home. In the past, I traveled fo work and had to spend an average of a week a month i hotels. That got old fast. But just sneaking away for a coupl of days for a nice break? I'm all about that.

When we lived in Guatemala, I once had to take a five day trip to the United States for a series of meetings, and relished the prospect of a few days out of my regular rou tine. The boys felt disappointed at not getting to come wit me, but they made up for it by sending a shopping list along They made sure I left room in my suitcase to bring back bag of Starbursts, boxes of frosted animal crackers, and the lates collection of *Diary of a Wimpy Kid* books. The trip started un eventfully. My flight landed in Kansas City. I picked up m rental car and headed straight for my first stop—Chick-Fil-A Priorities, right? Once I filled up on tasty chicken nugget crispy waffle fries, and lemonade, I drove to Target.

Holding my shopping list in one hand and steering m cart with the other, I found the American goodies I'd bee sent after. That's when I heard a child's voice. "Dad!"

I jumped, turned around, and looked in all directions. Even though my children were fifteen hundred miles away in nother country, at the sound of a child calling out my name, was ready to help.

My reaction reminded me of God. No matter how far way from God we've wandered, we can still call out His ıame. And when we do, He jumps right in to help us. God loes not wait for us to make an impossible journey to Him ny more than I would have expected my elementary-age ids to make the fifteen-hundred-mile journey from western Guatemala to Kansas City. Instead, God makes the journey o us. He expects us to call out to Him. You don't have to do nything special. Just call out His name, and He will answer ou. He's hyper-ready to respond.

—HOLLAND

Father, I call on You to help me today as I seek Your will for my family and our lives.

I'll Fly Away

Say to those who are fearful-hearted, "Be strong, do not fear! Behold, your God will come with vengeance, with the recompense of God; He will come and save you."

ISAIAH 35:4 NKJV

"Noah made it—he's in the top ten!" Our friend Pam a professional storyteller, broke the news—my so had been named one of the top youth storytellers in th nation, qualifying to represent Kentucky at the Nation Youth Storytelling Showcase in Provo, Utah. We were excite at the opportunity but nervous, as we would have to fly to th event and neither of us had flown before.

Noah's fear grew as we got closer to departure day. friend agreed to take us to the airport, three hours from ou home. Unbeknownst to me, during the long drive, Noah wa posting to social media on his phone.

"I'm REALLY scared—PRAY!"

"I don't know if I can do this! I NEED PRAYER NOW!"

He almost hyperventilated when we took the exit off th interstate toward the airport. Once there, we made it throug security and reached our gate an hour early, with Noah sti pleading online for divine intervention. Finally, the tim came to board and, to my surprise, he chose the window sea I'd figured he would not want to look down at all.

Noah closed his eyes and gripped the seat during takeof

out soon the flight attendant soothed him with peanuts, cookies, and a soft drink. He peered out the window and marveled at the closeup view of the clouds. That initial flight was a short connector, less than an hour. Upon landing, I asked Noah how he was doing.

"Great! Flying is the only way to travel!"

I laughed to myself and thanked God for answered prayer. Noah was fine during the four-hour flight to Utah, and we had a blast during the event. The trip back was uneventful, as we were veteran flyers by then.

The whole experience reminded me of the old adage that fear is False Evidence Appearing Real. Noah had stirred himself up, but in the end, discovered that flying wasn't scary at all.

If I need help in the face of fear, I turn to the book of Isaiah, as many verses there offer reassurance from a loving Father. God tells us not to fear because of who He is, and He explains what He will do if we lean into Him instead of the fear: He will help us, strengthen us, and uphold us. He often reminds me of this promise when I feel scared and unsure.

It is a wonder what prayer and snacks can do for a smooth flight through life.

—CARLTON

Lord, remind me of who You are so
I do not have to fear. You've got this!

If I am an effective father it is because I have devoted myself to become an instrument and model of human experience to my children.

GORDON MACDONALD

Let Him First Be Shaved

They shall not make any bald place on their heads.

LEVITICUS 21:5 NKJV

One Sunday morning when we lived in Guatemala, I was scheduled to speak at two churches in different services. Wanting to look presentable, I decided to buzz my hair down to the stubble, which even then was a better idea than my other choice—the notorious comb-over. The trouble started when I couldn't see in the foggy mirror at home.

"John-Paul, will you see if I left patches of hair?" I asked my youngest son.

"Just little fuzzy stuff to wash out,¨ he replied.

I washed and drove to church, where I checked the rear-view mirror. My head was a patchy mess of bald spots and prickly hairs. ¨I cannot get up there like this!"

My mother, who lived with us, suggested I buy a razor "to even it out." After a frantic search, I found an open drugstore with razors and locked myself in the church bathroom, an actual bathroom complete with a cast-iron, clawfoot bathtub. Our church was a converted mansion from who-knows-what era of Guatemalan history.

There was no water in the sink. Fortunately, the bath-tub tap worked. I took one swipe with that flimsy, fifty-cent razor and left a hairless, bloody trail behind me. Great. I could hear the music leader practicing in the sanctuary, so I poked my head around the door and caught her boyfriend's eye. Jon came over, looking concerned at the sight of me with a towel wrapped around my head. I explained, and Jon finished shaving my head. "You need some cream if you don't want razor rash." I bought the moisturizer, applied it, gave my two talks, and breathed a sigh of relief—until I reached up and found a large scab on my head. No wonder I had held two congregations in rapt attention that morning.

Ever have one of those days where you'd just like to hide? You can let the stress get to you, or you can decide to laugh it off. I think God appreciates a sense of humor. And your family will too.

—HOLLAND

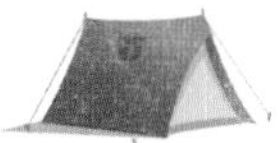

Father, when crazy days happen,
thank You for a sense of humor.

A Way with Women

So I concluded there is nothing better than to be happy and enjoy ourselves as long as we can.

ECCLESIASTES 3:12 NLT

Many dads like to go hunting and fishing with their children, but how many fathers have taken their sons to a women's ministry conference? I know only one—me.

Through a series of wacky circumstances only possible through God, Kathy and I became acquainted with Christian comedienne/singer Kay DeKalb-Smith. Kathy had ordered Kay's video as a gift for me after I saw her perform on television. Weeks passed, but the video failed to arrive. When we inquired, Kay realized she had forgotten to complete the order, so she mailed it right away, with extra goodies. Then she invited our family to be her guests at a women's conference she was scheduled to headline about an hour from our house.

We endured stares and curious looks from the women as we entered the church. I fully expected someone to point and say, "Not one of us!" One lady approached us and informed me the men's restroom on the main floor had been designated for women during the event, so my sons and I would have to use the one in the basement if nature called. A warm welcome, indeed.

The program began with a group song declaring "I'm Proud to Be a Woman," complete with hand motions. Kay hen took the stage and, after her opening number, peered out nto the audience.

"Carlton Hughes, is that you?"

All eyes were on me as I waved and answered, "Yes!" Kay explained we were there at her invitation, and with her seal of approval, the audience seemed to breathe a sigh of relief. From that moment on, the ladies warmed up and treated us with hospitality, doting on my boys. We had a great day of laughter and fellowship.

Why take your sons to an event like that? To show them life is a gift to be enjoyed. I have found good, hearty laughter does wonders when I am going through the inevitable trials of everyday living. Jesus Himself used humor in many messages—has anyone tried to stuff a camel through the eye of a needle lately?

The world needs more laughing Christians whose joy is evident even in the hard times. My family and I sure have our funny moments, even if we do have to take a break in the basement now and then.

—CARLTON

Father, lighten me up so I demonstrate the joy of salvation to others in this hurting world.

For the Paperboy

Every good gift and every perfect gift is from above, and comes down from the Father of lights.

JAMES 1:17 NKJV

Remember the day people stopped treating you like a cute little kid? For my oldest son, that sad day came on October 31, 2012. It was our first fall in a new small town, and we weren't sure what to expect from the neighbors with regard to trick-or-treating. But when dusk started to fall, the streets swelled with costumed children clutching empty bags. Quickly patching together a costume, Geoffrey snatched up a pillowcase and headed out for his piece of the action.

It wasn't long before he was back, though. The neighbors had happily filled the bags of the lisping princesses and various Marvel characters. But Geoffrey had hit a growth spurt and he didn't quite look like a kid anymore. So he had about seven pieces of candy for all his begging.

We had a disappointed boy that night. And of course, I felt so bad for him.

Everything changed the next day, though. He burst into the house in the middle of his paper route, grinning from ear to ear and holding a gigantic bag of chocolate bars with a note inside that read, "For the paperboy." That kid's grin was worth every chocolate bar I watched him eat over the next few days. He learned things had a way of working out in his favor. There were enough chocolate bars in that bag to keep Willy Wonka in business for a hundred years.

Like Geoffrey, I'm often denied the things I want. Friends I used to count on disappear. Money gets spent. Churches change. Things God used to give me without my asking don't come my way anymore. When that happens, I grow disappointed and frustrated because I forget that God's gifts—though they change—are still good and still perfect. They may come in a different package or in a different way than I expect, but they always provide more than enough.

—HOLLAND

Father, amid disappointments, help me remember that You give good gifts at the right time.

By Faith, My Noah

By faith Abraham obeyed when he was called to go out to the place which he would receive as an inheritance. And he went out, not knowing where he was going.

HEBREWS 11:8 NKJV

When Noah was four years old, he wanted a huge kitchen playset, complete with a sink and appliances, for Christmas. He admired it every time we went to the store, wrote a detailed letter to Santa, and reminded us often.

"I want that kitchen!"

At the time, when you asked Noah what he wanted to be when he grew up, he would answer "a chef." He planned to open a restaurant called "Noah's Soufflé" where the entire family would work; he even designated younger brother Ethan as the dishwasher. Brotherly love is a wonderful thing.

My brother-in-law found out about Noah's kitchen request and asked to buy the set for him. Since we would be celebrating with that side of the family on Christmas Eve, my wife and I agreed.

The big day arrived, and once all the presents under the tree were opened, my brother-in-law retreated to the garage and returned with the set wrapped in a large blanket. Noah did a grand unveiling, squealed with delight, and ran straight to my father-in-law, a preacher.

"Pop, I had faith I would get that kitchen! I prayed and ad faith!"

The whole extended family marveled at the faith of a mall child as he "cooked" us a feast of fake food.

I recently finished a Bible study of Abraham's life and vas encouraged by his simple yet strong faith. Much like my on, who had faith in something he could not see, Abraham onsistently believed God, even when the next step was clear s mud. If God said, "Go," he went. If God said, "Stay," Abe tayed. Either way, he had faith in the God who held all he answers.

Need a kitchen? Have faith!

—CARLTON

Father, give me the faith of a child,
for the little things as well as the big ones.

A Long, Strange Trip

When I was a child, I spoke and thought and reasoned like a child. But when I grew up, I put away childish things.

1 CORINTHIANS 13:11 NLT

I don't know when I became a man. Some days, I still fee like a little kid. I'm pretty sure I know the day my da became a man, though. He was twelve years old. Life wa very different for his generation than it is today.

My dad's dad served as a country doctor in souther Kentucky. Every day, he was busy, driving his Model T For through the hills and hollers to deliver babies, stitch up cut and treat diseases that don't even exist anymore, thanks to th miracles of modern medicine.

One day, someone appeared at the house, shouting abou an emergency. My grandfather thrust my dad into the ca in case he needed help, and they drove to the patient's farm There, they found a young woman bleeding profusely fron the neck. Her drunken husband had slashed her throat.

Gently easing his patient into the back of the Model T my grandfather told my twelve-year-old dad to jump in th driver's seat and head for Glasgow and the closest real hospi- tal. With my grandfather holding the woman's injured nec together, they set off on the forty-five-mile trip. Dad had t drive through the creek beds because there were no roads i r out of that part of Kentucky back then. It took them twelve hours to make the trip. The young woman survived.

I say Dad became a man that day because he did something so hard it seemed impossible, something that had life-or-death significance. To succeed, he had to leave behind childish thinking that focuses on self and put all his intelligence and grit into doing a job far too big for him. Someone's life depended on his success.

Are you facing an impossible task? Are you too young, inexperienced, or ill-equipped for the job? Ask God for grit. Then with His power, go do whatever you have to do for your faith, your family, or your job.

—HOLLAND

Father, grant me the grit to do hard things that help others.

Asleep at the Wheel

He makes me to lie down in green pastures;
He leads me beside the still waters.

PSALM 23:2 NKJV

Spring had sprung in our neck of the woods. It wa the first sunny day after a hard winter, and I had s much to do, I had so much to do, I truly was—as the sayin goes—running around like a chicken with its head cut off.

I arrived at work early to finish a project, taught on campus classes, and then drove several miles to teach anothe class at the county high school. With added worries abou my wife's health, our finances, and my boys' adjustments t new schools, I was physically and mentally spent. I finishe my high school duties forty minutes before Ethan's middl school down the street was scheduled to dismiss.

I drove to the middle school and took my place in th pickup line. It was unusual for me to be there early, so I turne off the car and leaned back in my seat. It was a beautiful after noon, not too hot and not too cold. In the first calm momen of that stressful day, I closed my eyes and promptly fell aslee

Thirty minutes later, the school bell jolted me awak At first, I didn't recognize where I was, until I saw childre racing toward their parents' vehicles. I was horrified that had fallen asleep at such an inopportune place and time, ye disappointed because the best rest I'd had in weeks had been interrupted by a stupid bell. But it was okay—the renewed energy I'd gained from the impromptu nap helped me as I got my son, returned home, and completed my tasks for the rest of the day.

That day years ago, God provided a brief respite from the fast lane of life. It's hard to slow down in this hectic world, but God not only commands rest, He promises to calm us Himself if we'll cooperate. If God rested after creating the world and Jesus retreated to quiet places to recharge, how much more do you and I need a break, even if it is in the school pickup line?

—CARLTON

Father, lead me to quiet places so I can rest in You.

Bad Medicine

Satan went out from the presence of the LORD*, and struck Job with painful boils from the sole of his foot to the crown of his head.*

JOB 2:7 NKJV

You'd probably feel pretty lucky to have a doctor for a dad if you were a kid. After all, if you would break an important body part or slice one open, there'd be someone around to patch you up. My dad had that privilege, his dad served as a country doctor early in the twentieth century. When Dad was about eleven years old, however, I think he'd have preferred a less direct approach to his medical issues. That year, he developed a severe boil.

Now, most boils aren't a big problem. Even severe ones that tend to stick to your rear end where they make sitting uncomfortable allow you to go about your other activities with no problem. My dad's boil, however, had festered on the bottom of his foot, making walking painful. This pretty much disabled him as a useful hand around the place.

So he limped to his bedroom and lay down on his bed barefoot. He spent the morning gazing out the window, lost in a daydream. My grandfather, I'm told, strode into the room holding a knife. He seized my dad's ankle, turned his foot over, and lanced the boil with one slash of his blade. I don't even want to think about how much that must have hurt.

But this unwelcome bit of surgery had to happen. Vithout it, my dad could have been lying around in bed or imping painfully from place to place for weeks, waiting for he boil to heal on its own. It was a relatively little pain that aved him from a lot of time and frustration later.

Has your Father ever performed an unwanted, unwel-omed, surprising bit of surgery on you? God has done it to ne a time or two. Just when I was getting ready to stretch ut for a few lazy days of daydreaming, God appeared with metaphorical knife, snatched me up by the ankle, and per-ormed some much-needed surgery.

Is He doing something in your life right now that hurts? Something surprising and painful? Remember Hebrews 12:5–6, "My son, do not make light of the Lord's discipline, nd do not lose heart when he rebukes you, because the Lord lisciplines the one he loves, and he chastens everyone he ccepts as his son" (NIV).

—HOLLAND

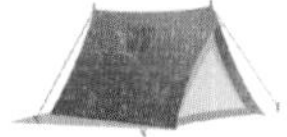

Father, help me learn and grow from painful events, trusting You through everything.

Make me, kind Lord, a worthy father,
hat I may lead my sons and daughters
In pathways ever fair and bright,
that I may guide their steps aright.

Tracking My Son

Be sure of this: I am with you always,
even to the end of the age.

MATTHEW 28:20 NLT

Noah was on the track team during his freshman year of high school. I taught a class there that year too. The arrangement was supposed to make it easy for me to attend his meets, but it did not always work out that way.

One important meet was scheduled at another school about an hour away. That morning, before I left for class, I gathered the items my family would need for the meet.

No one tells you when your kid signs up to run track that the meets are endless. The routine is the same for each event: first call for participants, followed by a second call, and then the one you've been waiting for—last call. At one site, there was even a fourth call.

"Would the runners for the home team report to the track *right now*?"

The athletes finally line up, the gun is sounded, and they're off! The actual race takes a minute or two, and then the process starts all over—first call, second call…you get the picture. And Noah always ran the two-miler, the last race.

I arrived at school that morning with my car loaded down with snacks, drinks, and books to pass the time at the meet, but during the last period of the day, it rained buckets. The track meet was cancelled, rescheduled a couple of days later

I packed everything again, went to school prepared, another downpour.

After two weeks of monsoon season, the clouds parted, and the sun came out in full force—on a day I had an important work meeting I could not miss. I was more disappointed than Noah, who shrugged it off.

At times like these, I depend on God to be with my children when I can't. He promises over and over to be with us and to watch over us, and I take Him at His word. God builds my trust that He will watch over my children, and He builds my boys' faith in a loving Father who is there all the time.

Anyone up for a track meet? I have snacks and an extra book or two to read.

—CARLTON

Father, I trust You to watch over my children even when I cannot be there for them.

Doing Battle with the Librarian

Learn to do right; seek justice. Defend the oppressed.
Take up the cause of the fatherless;
plead the case of the widow.

ISAIAH 1:17 NIV

I had my Martin-Luther-King-Jr. moment when the boys were eleven and twelve years old.

Have I mentioned that my sons are both black, and I'm white? As a family configuration, it's not unheard of, but it's not common either. Still, we've had this arrangement for so long that we forget how it can look to others. So none of us were quite prepared for what happened when we moved to a rural community in a midwestern state.

As a book person, I know the most important card in my wallet is my library card. As soon as I had a driver's license in our new state, the boys and I popped down to the library to get our cards. I handed the documents to the librarian and asked for a card for myself and a kid's card for each of the boys.

The librarian looked at the papers and then at the boys. "They're black."

I bit back my first answer and opted for a more diplomatic one. "Yes. And…?"

She looked at me as if I were a dolt and began to explain. The long and short of it was that black children didn't get library cards in that town without submitting a stack of additional documentation exclusively required for nonwhite people.

I don't recall ever having felt angrier in my life. I surely don't even need to say that we got the cards without submitting any more forms and without my having a coronary. But barely.

Dad, sometimes you need to stand up and fight for your kids. The biblical prophets cried out for God's people to do justice, to stand up for the oppressed, and to identify with the weak and powerless. If you know your kids are facing injustices and oppression, let them know you have their backs. Pray about it and then address it.

—HOLLAND

Father, give me wisdom to know if and how to intervene when my children face injustice.

Tennis (and Gout), Anyone?

What man is there among you who, if his son asks for bread, will give him a stone?

MATTHEW 7:9 NKJV

Ethan had played basketball in middle school but wanted to try something new in high school—tennis. Professional lessons were not an option in our rural area, so Ethan did what any other kid of his generation would do: he went to YouTube.

He watched videos on serving, keeping score, and delivering fancy spin moves—but to truly learn the game, he needed to practice every day. And there was only one person willing and able to help: Dad to the rescue!

When my sons were young, we went to the courts and batted the ball around, with efforts more akin to *America's Funniest Home Videos* than the US Open. This time, Ethan taught me the ins and outs of the game until we were playing some competitive matches. He progressed nicely, and I enjoyed our time together…until I suffered a gout attack.

Imagine someone beating your foot with a sledgehammer—that's gout. I was bedridden for days but longed to continue helping my son with something he wanted so badly. As soon as I was able to hobble, we returned to the courts. I stood in one spot while he practiced serving and batting balls at me. We were back in *AFV* territory, but at least I was doing something.

With much practice and study, Ethan made the high school tennis team as a freshman. He worked hard on his game through the following years, earning the number-one seed by the time he was a senior and playing in college for a while. His skills far outgrew mine, until one day, I asked if he wanted me to go to the courts with him. Shaking his head, he declared, "Dad, you're no longer competition for me."

God constantly worked behind the scenes to provide for Ethan, moving through every circumstance, even my painful gout, to make his tennis dreams come true. God, the ultimate Father, blesses our children with gifts so much better than what we can give.

I wanted something good for my child, to see him succeed in a sport he desperately wanted to play. Yet as much as I love my children, God loves them even more.

—CARLTON

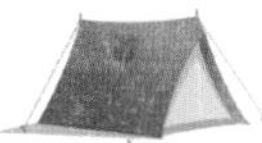

Father, I look for the good gifts in life today and thank You for them.

Relentless

The kingdom of heaven is like a merchant seeking beautiful pearls, who, when he had found one pearl of great price, went and sold all that he had and bought it.

MATTHEW 13:45–46 NKJV

"I want a medieval sword."

We were in England. Geoffrey was fifteen years old, and this trip was my Hail Mary pass at restoring our fractured relationship. At that point, I'd have tried to secure a knighthood for the kid if I thought it meant it might turn things around.

"Let's ask about the sword," I told him. We mentioned it to a friend of mine we'd met for dinner in Oxford.

"We're very antiblade in this country right now, I'm afraid." She shook her head. "Unless you pluck one off the walls of a castle, you'll have a hard time finding anything like that while you're here."

Never one to be dissuaded by such insignificant things as expert opinions, Geoffrey kept bugging me about getting him a sword. Historic castles? Meh. Winding streets lined by thatched cottages? Yawn. Ancient Roman edifices? Shrug. That boy had one thing on his mind: a medieval-style sword.

At Stonehenge, Geoffrey glanced at the world-famous rocks before suggesting we check the gift shop for a sword. They didn't have any, but the man there told us that a nearby attraction might carry some swords. Could we get there in the fifteen minutes left before it closed? My skills at navigating

British roads from the left side weren't great, but I said we'd give it a shot.

Sure enough, we pulled up just before they locked the door. Can you believe that gift shop was a veritable museum of medieval weaponry?

We still have the sword Geoffrey bought as a reminder of our trip, but also as a reminder of how far we've come together, and the importance of perseverance. Nothing deterred Geoffrey from wanting to find a place where he could get his hands on a medieval-style blade.

Jesus showed that same stick-to-it-iveness when He searched for me. Like a shepherd hunting for a sheep, a woman for a lost coin, a man for a lost son, or a fifteen-year-old in search of a sword, Jesus pursued me relentlessly. That's how He pursues you and your family too. And Jesus always finds what He seeks.

—HOLLAND

Father, thank You that You never gave up the search for me. Keep searching for my lost family members until all have been found.

Bumping Up Brotherly Love

He kissed all his brothers and wept over them,
and after that his brothers talked with him.

GENESIS 45:15 NKJV

My "memory" on social media this morning featured a favorite photo of my sons together, taken six years ago during a vacation in Pigeon Forge, Tennessee.

My family and I were enjoying a fun-filled afternoon at an adventure park, racing go-karts, playing arcade games, and challenging each other in miniature golf. As we walked around looking for our next activity, the boys discovered something new: bumper boats. It's the same concept as bumper cars, only on the water. Each boat was equipped with a high-powered squirt gun, so you could spray your prey as you were bumping them.

Noah and Ethan chased each other all over the small pool, alternately bumping and squirting each other with reckless abandon. They roared with laughter as they took out their sibling frustrations in the water. In the picture, they're grinning fiendishly in a momentary pause in the battle.

Observing my boys has taught their only-child dad about the whole sibling relationship. They have taken great joy in tormenting, picking at, and teasing each other; they ave fought worse than cats and dogs. But they've also had un playing video games together and talking sports. For me, here's nothing greater than hearing my sons laugh and carry on when they're actually getting along.

No story covers the gamut of brotherly rivalry and love ike the tale of Joseph. His brothers' jealousy caused them o do a heinous thing to their sibling, but God used their ctions to put Joseph's future into motion, to get him in the ight place at the right time so he could step into his divine lestiny. In the end, Joseph forgave his brothers and saved hem from famine and poverty. The picture of Joseph weeping when he reconciles with his brothers is one of the most bittersweet scenes in the entire Bible.

My boys may fight and argue, but I hope they always orgive and love as Joseph did.

—CARLTON

Father, guard the sibling relationship of my children so they will love each other no matter what.

Parachuting by Faith

The LORD, who delivered me from the paw of the lion and from the paw of the bear, He will deliver me from the hand of this Philistine.

1 SAMUEL 17:37 NKJV

"Dumbest thing I ever did."

That's what Geoffrey texted me the first time he jumped out of an airplane at the US Army Airborne school. The first jump was the scariest, he said. After that, he knew for sure the parachute would open and break his fall. Well, he was pretty certain it would catch him, anyway. One sergeant didn't jump with enough force, and his parachute pack scraped against the side of the plane. It didn't open for a long, long time while the man hurtled toward hard earth. Geoffrey said they heard him hit the ground.

"*Was he okay?*" I asked.

"He was limpin' pretty bad," Geoffrey said, nonchalantly biting into a chicken strip. "It was his fourth jump, though, and you gotta do five."

"So did he jump again?"

"Yep, nobody's going to get that close and give up just 'cause their parachute almost didn't open."

Of course not. Silly old Dad, prizing life and limb over the chance to wear a red Army Airborne beret.

No matter how many people tell you that your parachute will open, your first jump still feels incredibly stupid. But once you learn to trust your equipment, you'll feel free to give it all you've got. In fact, it's safer that way.

In the Bible, David's first encounter with a fearsome enemy wasn't his high-stakes standoff with Goliath. Rather, David first faced a mountain lion. Defeating the lion gave David proof that God would defend him. After the lion, David fought a bear. Again, God proved Himself faithful by delivering David.

So when he challenged the seasoned warrior Goliath in the Valley of Elah to single combat, David wasn't acting on blind faith. On the contrary, David was relying on the sure faith he'd developed as he had watched God deliver him from enemies in the past. God had been building David's confidence—along with those vital slingshot skills—for years.

Are you facing a giant of a problem? Afraid God can't or won't handle it? Look back. Remember. Has God faithfully delivered you in the past? Then, surely, He will not fail you now.

—HOLLAND

Father, give me eyes of faith to see Your work in my past and to trust my present and future into Your hands.

What Was That Word?

Give honor to marriage, and remain faithful to one another in marriage.

HEBREWS 13:4 NLT

What if someone gave you a gift that could cause repercussions if you used it improperly? Yeah, I'm talking about the "s" word. *Sex*. Now, I have your attention.

As my sons neared adolescence and started noticing girls I knew it was time for "the talk," something I had been dreading. How could I discuss such a personal thing with these boys?

I wondered and prayed about how to approach the subject when someone—I can't remember who—gave me a CD with teachings about the "s" word from a youth minister. I listened and found it to be a sound, simple explanation of not only the birds and the bees but also the spiritual aspects of saving yourself for marriage. The speaker had a slight speech impediment, but the message was so good, it didn't bother me.

I decided to use the CD as a discussion starter, playing it in the car as I toted the boys to a sports practice or to a school event. My first victim was Noah, who tried to shrink into the seat as I played the message during a long trip. He had no questions afterward, so I figured I'd accomplished that mission.

A few months later, it was Ethan's turn as we followed the bus carrying Noah and his teammates to a track meet. Ethan's response was much the same as his brother's—shrinking into the seat, no discussion when it was over. The bus stopped at a convenience store, so we followed. Ethan bolted from the car, found his brother, and began whispering something to him. Noah howled with laughter and yelled so loudly everyone in the parking lot could hear him.

"*Thex*! You had to listen to the *thex* CD!"

The speech impediment—that was their focus, what they heard. Still, I trust the point was made.

Many voices in culture try to lead our children one way, but our job as their parents is to teach them God's way, no matter how uncomfortable or unpopular it may be. God gives us good gifts and instructions on how to use them. We should be the ones sparking the discussion with our kids on matters such as thex—er, *sex*.

—CARLTON

Father, give me courage to teach my children Your ways.

There is nothing higher and stronger and more wholesome and useful for life in later years than some good memory, especially a memory connected with childhood, with home. Those who carry many such memories with them into life are safe to the end of their days.

FYODOR DOSTOEVSKY

The End

Jesus said to her, "I am the resurrection and the life. He who believes in Me, though he may die, he shall live. And whoever lives and believes in Me shall never die. Do you believe this?"

JOHN 11:25–26 NKJV

Just half a year has passed since I saluted my oldest son, Geoffrey, farewell when he turned soldier and left home. My mother is dealing with the debilitating effects of her age and health. I'm the strong, sane one around the place now, which ought to tell you something.

Someday, probably sooner than I would like, John-Paul, my youngest son, and I will be left alone to rattle around the house, fussing at the dogs and getting on one another's nerves like two crotchety old geezers. One day, I'll bid goodbye to our dogs too. And eventually, John-Paul will make his own independent way forward. He and Geoffrey will have to get themselves out of whatever trouble they get into. Although based on the number of phone calls—and guess who called just as I was typing that sentence…ahem.

In my less morbid moments, I plan what I'll do next: dust off ambitions I shelved during my mother's illness and my children's last years of adolescence. I may achieve new goals in the coming years, but after this year, nothing in my life will ever be the same again.

My friend, if you live long enough, you'll wave goodbye to the people you love too. College. The military. The mission field. A move. A ministry. They all can fray the ties that bind us together. Eventually, death itself will sever you from the ones you love the most, leaving you without their comforting presence until heaven.

Here's the most important thing I can say to you about heaven: Be there. Let nothing prevent you from showing up in God's kingdom, not your bad experiences with church, not your questions about the Bible, not your fears about what you'll have to give up to follow Jesus. Nothing. Don't hold back from the hope of eternal life with God that begins here and now and goes on forever. Maybe this is a good time to decide whom you'll follow. As for me, I will follow Jesus—all the way home.

—HOLLAND

Father, I choose now to follow Jesus.

Turning 50 and Letting Go

Like arrows in the hand of a warrior,
so are the children of one's youth.

PSALM 127:4 NKJV

I had to let go right before my fiftieth birthday.

I didn't let my hair down for a night on the town. (What hair?) I didn't purchase a midlife-crisis sports car. (Like I could afford one of those.) I didn't even sing a karaoke version of "Don't Stop Believin'" with a lampshade on my head. (Now, would I do that? Well…maybe.) No, the day before my big day, I dropped my firstborn off at college.

Noah had chosen to attend my alma mater. It was a surreal experience for me to be back on campus, walking the same sidewalks and halls thirty years later. Once we'd moved him into the dorm, we went to lunch at my all-time favorite Italian restaurant, a few blocks from the university.

As we finished delicacies that tasted just like they had back in the good old days, my wife made an excuse to slip away. She returned with a surprise, a chocolate birthday cake—another favorite of mine, from the bakery next door. The family had conspired and ordered it the day before.

"I'm not going to be there on your birthday, so we had to do something," said Noah.

I fought back tears as we enjoyed the decadent dessert. He and Ethan gave me a gift, *Pat Benatar's Greatest Hits* CD. They knew me too well; I had tormented—er, entertained—them with her songs during many long car trips.

After lunch, I went through a wrinkle in time as I jammed to "Love Is a Battlefield" while cruising through campus like it was 1984. Only it was 2014, and I was leaving my son and driving a hundred miles back home.

Letting your child go is not easy, but it is part of God's plan. From the time they are born, it is our duty to steer our kids on the right path, training them up so they can chart their own course. We are to aim them at the world as arrows, ready to hit the mark for God's glory. I will always have concerns about my children that I will need to turn over to God, but I will pray for them and trust God to know what's best for them.

—CARLTON

Father, I yield my children to You and Your plan.

What Are You Doing Here?

In peace I will lie down and sleep, for you alone,
O Lord, will keep me safe.

PSALM 4:8 NLT

Geoffrey and John-Paul shared a bedroom in our small apartment in Guatemala. Their beds were supposed to be bunked, but the ceiling hung too low for that. So they slept in separate beds but side by side.

Their room also held a built-in closet with drawers and spaces to hang clothes. A long empty space with four doors ran across the top of the closet. I was never sure what to do with that space, but John-Paul came up with an inventive idea. He'd sleep up there, he said.

Umm…okay. I checked to make sure he couldn't fall out, an accident that could have been disastrous on the hard tile floor below. Sure enough, he would be entirely safe asleep in the top of his closet.

"It's going to be very dark in there, though," I said. "You'll have these little doors shut all night with no outside lights."

He seemed unfazed.

So the next night, we put a pillow and blanket in the top of the closet, and I boosted John-Paul up. He said goodnight and shut the door. I figured I'd hear a squall in the middle of the night, but not so much as a single peep came from the boys' room.

The next morning, I opened the closet doors, woke John-Paul, and lowered him out of his hiding place. "Sleep okay up there?" He nodded.

That night, however, he opted to return to his bed instead of sleeping in the top of the closet. I guess he'd had enough of the adventure and wanted a decent night's rest.

Like John-Paul, I've often craved new adventures, something to break the monotony of everyday life. Biblical characters such as Elijah and David certainly lived adventurous and even dangerous lives in God's service, but they also made time to rest and restore themselves.

Dad, take some time for adventure, but don't neglect your rest.

—HOLLAND

Father, help me get the rest I need to take proper care of myself and my family.

Keep on Truckin'

A man's heart plans his way,
but the LORD *directs his steps.*

PROVERBS 16:9 NKJV

"I found a truck online, Dad. Can you take me to see it?" Ethan had gotten his first real job making decent money, and he was itching to buy a vehicle.

"Where is it?"

"At a lot in Tennessee."

Ever the dutiful dad, I agreed to a wild-goose chase, an hour-and-a-half trip to check out this truck. Ethan's girlfriend, Kersyn, and his best friend, Matt, tagged along.

Ethan found the vehicle, a shiny red number, on the lot, and it was love at first sight. He and Matt examined it as the salesman approached. I discussed our price range with him, and he handed over the keys for a test drive.

Ethan and I climbed into the "dream truck," and he turned the key. Nothing. Tried again—no go. The salesman said it had been sitting on the lot for a while and might need a battery charge, so we looked around while he retrieved the charger from the office and hooked it up.

"It's a great truck! I can't believe they're selling it at such a low price!" Ethan was ecstatic as we browsed.

"Yes, if it would only *run*!" Sarcasm is my love language.

After a while, the salesman tracked us down to inform us the battery was fully charged. We returned to the vehicle and tried to start it, but it sputtered and died. The salesman tried charging again, to no avail. Despite several attempts, we were unable to move that truck, not even a foot. We admitted defeat and left the lot empty-handed except for a good story to tell. Ethan wasn't discouraged for long. He found a newer model—one that actually ran—closer to home a few months later.

Have you ever prayed for something you wanted so badly, but it didn't work out the way you thought it would? I heard somewhere that all of us will probably spend our lives *someplace else* doing *something other than* what we originally planned. There's a lot of truth in that.

There've been times I've been sure I knew exactly how God was going to answer a request—only to be surprised by His plan. God's way is always best, but I am often blinded to the good by my own desires. I receive the true blessings when I surrender to His will.

—CARLTON

Father, I surrender to Your plan, not mine.

Ain't Misbehavin' (Sometimes)

The younger son got together all he had, set off for a distant country and there squandered his wealth in wild living.

LUKE 15:13 NIV

Boys who misbehave in school make more money as adults than boys who follow instructions. That's based on research from Johns Hopkins University, and I'm pretty sure my own classmates from both elementary and middle school have largely borne it out.

It's sad news for me, though. I was a tediously well-mannered child. I could have decorated my room in "best behaved" and "most Christlike" awards. According to the research, I'm doomed to a life of mediocrity. On the flip side, my own children should have bright futures ahead of them.

Seriously, why do the bad kids seem to get it all? When I was in elementary school, one boy in our class was notorious for landing in trouble. Not a day went by when this kid didn't end up standing against the wall at recess, getting sent to the office, or carrying a note home to his parents. (By the way, I met his parents. They weren't the sort of people you'd want to take notes home to.)

I Googled this kid a couple of years ago, figuring I'd find out what prison he'd finally landed in. Instead, I discovered that he holds a swanky job at the US State Department. And me, the good boy the teachers all approved of? I write devotionals and clip coupons—hardly the equivalent of a high-ranking government post.

It's not fair. But then, grace isn't fair either. Most of Jesus's stories show the upside-down, totally unfair nature of the kingdom of God. In that realm, boys who set off for a far country or who became tax collectors or did something else wicked were the ones God seemed to have a soft spot for. And the good kids were the ones who got reamed out. Why?

Jesus knew we'd have to experience the strength of our wrongdoing in order to appreciate the greater power of His grace. When I watch people I love make self-destructive choices, I remember that they are just the kind of people Jesus made the heroes of His stories.

—HOLLAND

Father, give me Your eyes to see past the action of the moment into what You are doing for eternity.

Drive, He Said

Rejoice in our confident hope. Be patient in trouble, and keep on praying.

ROMANS 12:12 NLT

If you need patience and an increased prayer life, teach your child how to drive.

Ethan had gotten his learner's permit and had been practicing his driving for a while. This wasn't my first rodeo—I'd taught Noah and my brothers-in-law years before, but it was still nerve-racking.

One evening, we had just enough time after school to get something to eat before Ethan's tennis match, so I picked up him and his friend, Brad, from the courts. Ethan begged me to let him drive to the restaurant in a nearby town. I reluctantly agreed, even though he didn't have much experience in traffic.

"Try to stay in your lane," I encouraged as he weaved a bit. "Ease off the gas, you're a bit too close to that car in front of us."

I prayed and tried to stay calm, but I had a death grip on the passenger-side door handle. "We need to turn here—use your signal now." I coached him through the maze of a shopping center parking lot leading to our destination.

"If you turn this way, you'll miss most of the traffic, and it will be easier to get where we're going," I said.

Brad had been quiet in the backseat but finally spoke up. "Boy, Mr. Hughes, you're patient. My mom would have been screaming her head off and trying to grab the wheel if that had been me driving. How do you do it?"

All I could answer was, "It's Jesus!"

I've heard people say not to pray for patience because you never know what you'll have to go through to get it. But patience is a fruit based on the acknowledgement that God will pull us through every situation. I have found the Lord gives it to me in the right amount, at the appropriate time, just when I need it.

When your child starts driving, take a deep breath, pray without ceasing, and hold on to that door handle for dear life.

—CARLTON

Lord, calm me in the tense situations of life.

Turnabout Is Fair Play

Fathers, do not exasperate your children.

EPHESIANS 6:4 NIV

Geoffrey began physical fitness training just before his fourteenth birthday. He was a little young for the heavy stuff, but his personal trainer got him started on bodyweight exercises, dumbbells, and a decent diet.

Geoffrey mourned over that diet. "No more pumpkin pie."

But he stuck with it. No matter what else happened, Geoffrey hit the gym every single day with single-minded devotion. And he got results.

Biceps grew, legs reshaped, and belly fat melted away. He was a walking, talking, weightlifting commercial for his personal trainer. And I was jealous. My own tiny biceps, spindly legs, and jelly-filled belly stood out beside his physique. I wanted a trainer too. But I couldn't horn in on Geoffrey's time, nor could I afford to pay a trainer for Geoffrey and then pay him again to train me. So I picked what I considered a cheap and effective alternative. "You could train me, Geoffrey."

He rolled his eyes and asked how much I would pay. I named a price, and he countered with a higher one. We finally negotiated a mutually disagreeable settlement. Then, he said I needed to quit eating pumpkin pie. I was already growing tired of this new trainer, and we hadn't even had our first session in the gym yet.

The next day, Geoffrey led me to the weight room like a lamb to the slaughter. Although knowledgeable and effective, my son grew easily frustrated, pushed too hard, and generally made working out not fun.

His harsh tone sounded uncomfortably familiar. I clearly heard echoes of me helping him with his homework—easily frustrated, pushy, and generally not fun. I was getting a taste of my own medicine, and it was nasty.

I wanted to deliver a lecture on respect and kindness. Instead, I decided to start showing it more and lecturing about it less. If Geoffrey felt like I did, it was time one of us changed how he talked, and the only person I could control was me.

The Bible instructs us dads not to exasperate our children. Exasperated children often become exasperating children, perpetuating a dysfunctional cycle. If someone in your family is exasperating you, maybe you could prayerfully consider how you are part of the problem. And change.

—HOLLAND

Father, show me how I may be exasperating my children. And help me change.

I know now that I was a child placed in the protection of my mother and father, and all that I learned about peace and nature and the size of the moon I learned in the backyard.

CHRISTOPHER DE VINCK

Rockin' the Bod

Man looks at the outward appearance,
but the Lord looks at the heart.

1 SAMUEL 16:7 NKJV

One day I opened the refrigerator to discover a can of biscuits that had popped open. Globs of dough were sticking out all around it.

Looks like my body, I thought as I cleaned the mess.

At my age, I am totally rocking the "dad bod," to the point that I could be the poster child for the look. I wear my cargo pants and shorts with pride, I favor black, and I hardly ever tuck in a shirt (because, well, *biscuits!*). I try to eat healthy and exercise, but it's hard at my age. I have accepted the fact I will never have a six pack except for the sodas I occasionally bring home. And I'm okay with it.

I earned this dad bod through years of being the household human garbage disposal—eating leftovers from my sons' plates…an extra chicken nugget here, a few fries there, a half-eaten piece of pizza on the side. Of course, I lost that status once the boys' hit their I'm-still-hungry-and-need-more-food adolescent years, but the damage was done.

I've enjoyed ice cream during nights out and all manner of snacks while playing cars on the floor. I've eaten more than my share of movie popcorn because every parent knows it's cheaper to buy the refillable large bucket (not to mention the refillable large soda). I have a condition known as "done-lap disease"—my belly has "done lapped" over my waistline. These pounds tell many stories.

I have a friend who explains, "God made our bodies as temples, but I'm special—He made me a *cathedral*!" Yep, that's me—just call me Notre Dame.

My wardrobe is not trendy at all, but clothes don't make this man. Neither do numbers on a scale define me. My identity is found in Jesus, in what He has done for me and who He says I am. Taking care of the body He gave me is something I need to work on, but being comfortable in my own skin is vital to my self-worth.

—CARLTON

Father, let me find my identity and worth in You.

I Gotta Go!

At the place where the road passes some sheepfolds,
Saul went into a cave to relieve himself.
But as it happened, David and his men were
hiding farther back in that very cave!

1 SAMUEL 24:3 NLT

As a kid, I wondered if Jesus ever needed to visit the bathroom. Then I got worried Jesus might not want me speculating about that.

I did discover, however, that at least one biblical character's plumbing worked properly—King Saul's. While out hunting for David, Saul happened to choose the very cave where David and his men were hiding to do his business. David had the king at his mercy—he could have ended Saul's life right then, but he did not.

But it's not just Bible characters who have weird bathroom stories. When the boys and I lived in Guatemala, we were excited to learn that IHOP had opened a store in the country's capital city. We decided we needed some of those internationally famous pancakes, so the three of us got up at 3:30 a.m. one morning and met my friend Brendan at the bus station for the four-hour ride from our city to the capital. About halfway there, the bus driver pulled over for a bathroom break. The boys opted to remain on the bus, but Brendan and I filtered out with the people walking through suspicious organic material on the ground to an outhouse with an iron bar that kept the door closed. I entered, carefully set the bar in place, and began what I was there to do.

Out of the corner of my eye, I glimpsed the bus—with the boys still on it—pulling out. Brendan yelped from the outhouse next to mine, and he and I came tearing out of those stalls, holding up our pants with one hand and waving with the other. Thankfully, the bus driver pulled over. I don't know what happened to the iron bar in the door, but I'd hate to have been the next person in line who had to find it in the suspicious organic material.

Every time I think of Brendan, or use a sketchy public restroom, I remember our adventures on that four-plus-hour trip for a stack of pancakes at IHOP. Sometimes the best memories with our kids can come from the most unexpected places. So get off your phone. Go places. Do things. Use the outdoor toilets. Be weird. Make memories that will last all their lives.

—HOLLAND

Father, give me weird moments with my kids,
times we can remember together for years to come.

Anything but Perfect

God's way is perfect.
All the LORD's promises prove true.

PSALM 18:30 NLT

Mistakes are an inevitable part of life, especially in the journey of parenthood. I could fill another book with them. Noah will never let me live down one of my biggest blunders.

My wife and I had a strict rule for our sons about school and church: you did not miss unless you were running a fever or throwing up. One morning, Noah woke up with the sniffles—he had a runny nose and some congestion but a normal temperature. We gave him some medicine and sent him off to school. He did fine but was dragging when he got home. The next morning he still had no fever and seemed a bit better, so back to school for him.

By midday, Noah felt worse, so even though his temperature remained normal, we took him to the doctor as a precaution. Imagine our surprise when test results showed he had walking pneumonia. How could we have missed that? I wanted to crawl under the examining table.

The doctor explained the particular strain of pneumonia Noah had did not always produce a fever, and he assured us we were not bad parents for sending him to school. He prescribed medicine and gave Noah an excuse to stay home from school for the remainder of the week, with instructions for him to drink plenty of fluids and get some rest. At the pharmacy, I looked for a shirt with the scarlet letters *BP* for *Bad Parent*, but I couldn't find one. I did the next best thing, and purchased Noah a new "parental guilt" video game.

No parent is perfect. We make mistakes now and then, and we cannot beat ourselves up over them. God is the only perfect Father, and there are many things in life only He can do for our children. How else would they see their need for Him? From that point on, I prayed for help with my boys and asked God to fill in the gaps when I messed up. As the good Father he is, He's kept His promise.

—CARLTON

Father, inhabit the places where I fall short as a parent.

Hanging by a Thread

So do not fear, for I am with you; do not be dismayed,
for I am your God. I will strengthen you and help you;
I will uphold you with my righteous right hand.

ISAIAH 41:10 NIV

Ever find yourself literally hanging by a thread?

I have. Right after we moved to Guatemala, the boys talked me into visiting Panajachel, a village situated on the edge of the picturesque Lake Atitlán, which is ringed by volcanoes. The views are legendary.

We meandered around the town, grabbed some lunch, and turned down the option to purchase marijuana from several of the hippie-types who had made their homes by the lake. In the spirit of a peaceful day, we even toured a butterfly garden. And that's where Geoffrey spotted the fateful sign: Zip Lines This Way.

"Let's go ziplining!"

I agreed because I'd been on a zipline at a camp once. That line was anchored to the top of a hill about thirty feet high. No sweat, right?

The ziplines at Lake Atitlán were nothing like the ones at camp, let me tell you! These Guatemalan lines stretch from three hundred to a thousand feet each. You hang two hundred feet off the ground while sliding along, supposedly while gasping at breathtaking views. John-Paul wisely kept both feet on solid ground at the base camp, but Geoffrey was determined to go. I was equally determined not to let a nine-year-old kid outdo me. I nearly lost my lunch swinging over that lake. Two years later, the class of fifth graders that I work with took me ziplining in another location. My expression must have been just as dour that time around, since one of the boys said, "Mr. Webb, I thought you were going to pee yourself."

I thought I was too. And frankly, I had good reason. I was, after all, hanging by a literal thread, hundreds of feet off the ground!

Speaking of hanging by a thread, I'm managing life with two teens and an aging parent. Hanging by a thread perfectly describes my emotions at times. But God is a master weaver. His thread is tight and strong. It won't snap and drop us at a critical juncture, no matter how high off the ground we hang. We might nearly lose our lunch sometimes, but God never lets us fall.

—HOLLAND

Father, I feel like I'm hanging by a thread. Don't let me fall.

The Traditional Christmas Lard

A merry heart does good, like medicine.

PROVERBS 17:22 NKJV

A few years ago, my church started a new tradition at the annual Christmas party: a white elephant gift exchange. This game has many names—Dirty Santa, Dirty Bingo, Christmas Free-For-All (yes, I made that one up)—but they all have the same routine. Each person brings a gift, draws a number, and grabs the corresponding present under the Christmas tree. That person can either keep the gift or steal someone else's. It's great fun and, at our church, very competitive.

One year when Ethan was part of the teen youth group, he was excited about the game, wanting to choose just the right thing to take to the party. Our pastor had set a five-dollar price limit for the gifts, knowing most people would buy Christmas ornaments, what-nots, or other simple things. Ethan had noticed the previous year that gag gifts got the biggest response, so he went to the grocery store and purchased his item—a bucket of lard.

I helped him wrap the gift in a way that would disguise its contents, and my son proudly carried it to the party and placed it under the tree. Howls of laughter rang through the fellowship hall when an unsuspecting person opened a tub-o-fat. Ethan was in hog heaven (pun intended) and, after much give-and-take, somehow ended up with the lard back at the end of the evening.

It was inevitable some of my crazy would rub off on my children, and I was a proud papa. The Bible says a merry heart is like medicine to the soul, and I believe it.

Every day I have a choice—I can walk around with a frown, complaining about anything and everything, or I can smile, looking for the good in life. It is my prayer to spend more of my days smiling than complaining. I want to spread joy wherever I go, and I hope my boys choose to do the same.

Why not share some laughter medicine today? After all, it comes by the tubful.

—CARLTON

Father, let my joy be full and overflowing to those around me.

Letters in the Shadow of a Firing Squad

A good name is more desirable than great riches;
to be esteemed is better than silver or gold.

PROVERBS 22:1 NIV

Neither of my parents were sentimental. Some families tuck away albums stuffed with family photos, disk drives of videos, and recordings of personal stories. We have a few pictures squirreled away somewhere. I'm not sure where exactly.

In a rare show of sentiment, mother saved a recording of my father's voice for me. I listened to it once. In it, my dad delivers the most boring speech in the history of public addresses. If I remember it correctly, his whole message had to do with how many nights he'd left the lights on in his office. It's hardly a message of valor delivered from father to son.

Some families do better than we do when it comes to passing messages from one generation of men to the next. Like one of my personal heroes, the Filipino revolutionary Ninoy Aquino. I grew up in the Philippines just a few years after Ninoy faced his execution for standing up to the country's dictator, so I know the effect his life and death had on the nation and the people he loved.

When Ninoy sat in prison, accused of subversion, he wrote letters to his son who was then about twelve years old. In one of those letters, Ninoy said, "The only valuable asset I can bequeath to you now is the name you carry. I have tried my best during my years of public service to keep that name untarnished and respected, unmarked by sorry compromises for expediency. I now pass it on to you."

Ninoy was right. No matter how little wealth we have to hand down to our sons and daughters, we can always give them a good name. Such a gift might seem small in a world where family honor holds little currency, but the Bible often speaks of a good name or reputation. Shakespeare, in *Othello*, called a good name "the immediate jewel of [our] souls." How can you bequeath a good name to your son or daughter? What's your family's reputation? Is it something to hand down like a cherished jewel? Or do you have some work to do, polishing your family's name?

—HOLLAND

Father, help me earn a good name, one I can hand down to my children with satisfaction.

Doing Good in the 'Hood

He who has pity on the poor lends to the L*ORD,*
and He will pay back what he has given.

PROVERBS 19:17 NKJV

"I am volunteering for a summer program at a rescue mission in the city," Noah said. "I'll be there for two months. Can you drop me off?"

He dropped this bombshell on my wife and me at the end of his first year of college, which had not gone as planned. In fact, it had been so rocky that he'd decided to return home and attend the local community college the next year. But first, this mission project.

I was proud that my son wanted to help the poor, but I felt trepidation as well. The sinking feeling intensified when we dropped him off a few weeks later.

The program was designed for participants to experience what life was like for the disenfranchised, those with limited funds in less than desirable conditions. The provided apartment, to be shared with four other guys, was tiny and run-down. To say the urban neighborhood was rough is the understatement of the century. As I unloaded his belongings from my car, I was concerned for Noah's safety—and for my hubcaps.

Noah and his roommates received a small stipend that would barely cover food and minimal living expenses. I wanted to swoop in and save the day as Super Dad with money, groceries, and a pan of freshly baked brownies, but I wasn't allowed to—they had to survive on their own.

It was hard leaving my child in those conditions, but it ended up being a great learning experience for Noah. He emerged with an appreciation for the small blessings in life, a heart for the needy, and a keen sense of money management.

The experience taught me lessons as well. I learned God is faithful when we submit to His call, and He is pleased when we serve the "least of these" (Matthew 25:45). He reminded me that He can bring good out of anything, even a touchy situation in a rough area, and can be trusted to keep my child safe no matter where he may roam.

And He even watched over my hubcaps. You cannot beat protection like that.

—CARLTON

Father, open my eyes to ways I can serve the least of these, knowing You will watch over me as I do.

There is no more liberating experience than the joy of loving one's spouse and children, the confidence of being loved, and the knowledge that such love can move mountains and make nations whole.

GARY BAUER

God Bless VBS

Then, because so many people were coming and going that they did not even have a chance to eat, he said to them, "Come with me by yourselves to a quiet place and get some rest."

MARK 6:31 NIV

God bless VBS.

I never appreciated Vacation Bible School until I had little kids. The boys had lived at my house for about two months when I spied a sign at the local Baptist church. "Vacation Bible School Next Week from 6 to 9 Every Night: All Are Welcome."

Three child-free hours on my own each night for a week? The whole schtick sounded so good, I knew there had to be a catch somewhere. The boys were suspicious too. "Why are we going to that church instead of our own church?"

"We aren't actually going there," I explained 1,234 times. "We're just attending a special kids' thing this week."

They still glanced at me nervously. I had no idea they were so dedicated to our particular denomination. After the first night, though, their suspicions melted like an ice cream cone on the Fourth of July. In fact, they loved the whole week so much, I started hunting the town over for more VBS options. I found them among the Lutherans, Methodists, Nazarenes, two kinds of Pentecostals, and a variety of Baptists. My preschoolers got a theological smorgasbord of songs, games, and Bible stories. We became connoisseurs of VBS.

The best part of it all? I got some rest. Seriously, I'd drop off the boys at a fun-filled, Bible-based activity zone where I knew they'd have fun, then I'd kick back at home, watch my favorite shows, and enjoy junk food with no one begging me for a bite. My VBS gravy train came to an end when one of my kids bit a volunteer, but it was a treat while it lasted.

Dad, it's important to take a break. Kick back, watch your shows, eat junk food, or do whatever suits you. If you don't get some rest, your health will take a hit, your work will decline, and your family will suffer for it. God commanded times of rest and refreshing for a reason. Pack those kids off to VBS or another trustworthy activity, then follow God's command to get a little rest yourself.

—HOLLAND

Father, help me take advantage of opportunities to unwind and rest.

Comin' after Ya

For the Son of Man has come to seek and to save that which was lost.

LUKE 19:10 NKJV

Last Father's Day represented a transition of sorts, as it was my first one as an empty-nesting dad. Ethan had gotten married a week or so before, and he and his wife, Kersyn, had settled into an apartment three hours away from home. Both had steady jobs with not much time off. Noah was in college and working a summer job in the same general area, two hours away.

Their schedules would not accommodate a trip home, but I was not about to let the only holiday celebrating fatherhood pass without seeing my sons and new daughter-in-law. My wife and I took the only other option we had—we left home and went to them. It was the first of what will likely be many adventures chasing down our chicks who have flown the nest.

We arranged to meet in a town not far from both boys. We enjoyed lunch together at a nice restaurant, and I received gifts and an ice cream cake. As much as I love ice cream, especially in cake form, being with my family was the best thing about the day. Now that they are living on their own, I treasure time spent with my children like that.

My boys can move to the other side of the world from me, but I will still go after them. I am glad God does the same for me.

When I was a million miles away from Him, living a life far from His standard, He came after me anyway. To this day, when I stray and do things I should not be doing, God chases me down and gently brings me back into the fold. I am thankful for a Father who cares so deeply for me that He is not satisfied until I am safe with Him.

I will be that type of father for my boys, loving them no matter what they do and chasing them down no matter where they go.

—CARLTON

Father, continue to seek and to save me when I stray from You.

From the Front Lines

Peace I leave with you; my peace I give you.
I do not give to you as the world gives. Do not let
your hearts be troubled and do not be afraid.

JOHN 14:27 NIV

Just before my thirteenth birthday, my mother and I got caught up in a nine-day urban warfare that brought Manila to a standstill.

We had only lived in the Philippines for about six months and barely had our routine down. That morning, she walked me to the bus stop, and we looked at the nearly empty major highway.

"Something's wrong," Mother said.

An armed man came up from behind us and pointed. "You see those planes? They're bombing."

Alrighty then! My mother marched me home and turned on the radio. Sure enough, rebel soldiers had launched a coup attempt against the government. Some friends picked us up and took us to their home, which they believed would be safer.

They were wrong. The rebel soldiers moved in the same direction we did. My friend and I played war games in the front yard while crack-shot Filipino soldiers carried on a real and deadly war in the street behind the house.

Living on a battlefield felt kind of cool to a couple of twelve-year-old boys until someone moved a tank behind the house. When that thing fired, my friend and I tore across the yard and through the front door. If his dad hadn't held it open for us, we probably would've gone right through the glass.

Scary things happen in life. Your hometown may not lie in the middle of a war zone, but danger has a way of finding you no matter where you live. Accidents happen. Decisions go awry. People do foolish things. God gives us His peace for times like that. Peace is not something we get when we don't need it. Rather, it's something that comes to us only when we're afraid or in danger. During those times, we can turn to the one called the Prince of Peace and ask for help.

—HOLLAND

Father, please give me Your peace in the middle of things so frightening I can't even comprehend them.

Seasons Change

To everything there is a season,
a time for every purpose under heaven.

ECCLESIASTES 3:1 NKJV

When my children were babies, I would think, "Boy, will it be great when they are out of diapers and we can save money!" Then, "I can't wait until they can walk and I don't have to carry them all the time." And, "Won't it be cool when they can talk?"

Well, they moved past the diaper stage, but there were always other things to buy—the toys truly do get bigger and more expensive with each year. Both boys went straight from crawling to running, forcing me to chase them everywhere. Talking was yet another adventure, as it gave their sibling rivalry a whole new dimension.

I thought each phase of parenting would be easier, but that was seldom true. Preteen angst led to greater adolescent angst, and then driving—there's something to keep you on your knees. Before I knew it, the boys were off to college and on their own, and I was left with new feelings of loneliness and worry.

Now that my wife and I have been empty nesting for a while, I've gained some perspective. I miss my sons like crazy, but I know it's their time to forge their own paths in life and it's my time to trust God that what I taught them has stuck.

We've moved through a rite of passage, a finish line of sorts for the "growing up" stage of parenting.

My wife still gets wistful for the younger days. She'll see a couple with a baby and say, "I would go back to those days in a heartbeat!" Me? Dirty diapers and drool? No thanks, at least not until we have grandchildren.

The writer of Ecclesiastes meant business when he said there was a time for everything. Each season of parenting had its challenges, none easier than the other, just different. I learned I could wallow in the problems or I could enjoy the blessings along the way. I chose the latter.

—CARLTON

Father, watch over my children in each season of their lives.

A Letter from Basic Training

Trust in the Lord with all your heart, and lean not on your own understanding; in all your ways acknowledge Him, and He shall direct your paths.

PROVERBS 3:5–6 NKJV

Do you ever wonder how the story of your life as a dad will end? Is it all worth it? Will your efforts to help your kids grow up into not-incarcerated human beings ever bear fruit?

A child wandering in the proverbial far country can highlight your questions and your fears. *Was it my fault? Did I mess up so badly that this kid is ruining his life? Have I failed as a dad?*

Success is intimately woven into our cultural concept of masculinity—I'm a man, therefore I'm successful; if I'm unsuccessful, I must not be a man. Frankly, there's nothing I want to succeed at more than being a dad.

After my oldest son left for the army, he wrote me several letters from basic training. The first one consisted of two lines scrawled on a pocket notepad, but as training dragged on, the letters grew longer and fuller. After about six weeks, one arrived in the mailbox, and I eagerly ripped it open. I started reading it aloud to my elderly mother. After about two sentences, I got choked up and had to stop. Geoffrey had written to tell me how proud he was of finishing basic training, but he gave me the credit for helping him become the kind of person who could do that.

After years of hoping for a sign that my efforts hadn't been totally misdirected, I got what I wanted in his letter. I tucked away Geoffrey's note…somewhere. (I told you we're not sentimental people, but this I needed to hang on to.) It's my reminder that relationships are long. You can't stop at one point along the way and measure your failure or your success. Just keep going.

Trust that the God, whom Jesus called "Father," understands what it means to be a dad. His wisdom will guide you, and His grace will cover your mistakes and failures. Whether being a dad feels frustrating or rewarding right now, don't hold on to those feelings. Instead, hold on to the sure and steady hand of God. Need help being a dad? Here's my best advice, taken straight from Scripture: *Trust in the Lord.*

—HOLLAND

Father, help me to trust You in this journey of fatherhood, no matter what.

About the Authors

Carlton Hughes has spent hours chasing his two boys, Noah and Ethan, through the cross-country courses and tennis complexes of Eastern Kentucky. He has fixed boo-boos, carpooled numerous kids to practices, and weathered various trials with his now young adult sons. In his roles as communications professor at Southeast Kentucky Community and Technical College and children's pastor at Lynch Church of God, he has also served as a surrogate father for hundreds of kids.

Carlton has been published in numerous books, including *Chicken Soup for the Soul* and several devotionals from Worthy Publishing—*The Wonders of Nature*, *Let the Earth Rejoice*, *So God Made a Dog*, *Just Breathe*, and *Everyday Grace for Men*. An award-winning writer and speaker, Carlton is a founding blogger at AlmostAnAuthor.com, is a regular contributor at InspiredPrompt.com, and is a longtime planning committee member of Kentucky Christian Writers Conference. He and his wife, Kathy, are empty nesting in Cumberland, Kentucky, with a bunch of cats. Carlton tries to "find the funny in life and faith" in his writing.

In March 2004, **Holland Webb** received the life-changing phone call that he would be adopting two boys, ages three and four. Since that day, as a single dad, he's had several more life-changing phone calls—from the principal, the children's pastor, and the highway patrol. Holland couldn't be more proud of his boys, Geoffrey and John-Paul. They have found adventure in the mountains of Guatemala, the deserts of Morocco, and the cornfields of Iowa. They now live in South Carolina, where the boys are entering adulthood and Holland is entering his dotage.

A full-time freelance writer, Holland produces content for businesses, marketing agencies, and universities. He also writes for *Devozine* and *Keys for Kids* and cohosts a podcast called *The Afterword: A Conversation about the Future of Words.*

Carlton and **Holland** met at the Blue Ridge Mountains Christian Writers Conference and bonded immediately. When Carlton gave an exhausted Holland a place to stay one night, they did more talking than sleeping, and a friendship was born. Over the course of the event, they hatched the idea that became *Adventures in Fatherhood.*

Ellie Claire
Hachette Book Group
1290 Avenue of the Americas, New York, NY 10104

ellieclaire.com

First edition: April 2020

Ellie Claire is a division of Hachette Book Group, Inc. The Ellie Claire name and logo are trademarks of Hachette Book Group, Inc.

The publisher is not responsible for websites (or their content) that are not owned by the publisher.

Print book interior and cover design by Bart Dawson.

ISBN: 9781546014966

Printed in China

RRD-S

10 9 8 7 6 5 4 3 2 1